"Janet. Gillispie's story is one [ ]
unmitigated grace."   —CECIL M[ ]

"Raw and real. Janet's life is a massive tragedy seized by God's mammoth grace."   —HAROLD SIMON, physician

"An incredible story of God's love and grace."
—EMMA LAURA PATRICK,
retired director of children's education, Mountain Brook Baptist Church

An absolutely inspiring story of God's grace, a mother's love, and pure honesty."   —TOM COOK, DSW, ACSW,
Catholic Family Services

"Janet's story reminds us that it is never too late to change, that healing is possible, and that God's love is always available."
—CONNIE HILL, former Pathways director

"*Delivered* reminds me to never give up on anyone."
—YVAS WITHERSPOON, primary counselor, Olivia's House

"Inspiring to anyone recovering from problems with living due to addiction."   —REV. CHARLES H. MOZLEY, SCAC, NCAC 1,
Christian Counseling Services

"*Delivered* shows the destructive power of sin and the redeeming power of Jesus Christ."   —DR. RICHARD C. TRUCKS,
pastor, Third Presbyterian Church

"Authentic, insightful, and a must-read. . . . A riveting story of the horrific effects of addiction and the redemptive power of God."
— CATHY GILBERT MCELDERRY, PhD, MPH, LCSW, University of Alabama at Birmingham, Department of Social Work

"*Delivered* takes the reader down into the dark caverns of addiction and homeless street survival; then breaks through to a bright sustained mountain top experience. The contrast is stark, inspiring and nothing short of miraculous!" — DR. JOHN C. ZIEGLER, public information officer, Alabama Department of Mental Health

"Shocking, revealing, scary, sad, but with a happy ending. . . . A prime example of what can happen when God steps into a person's life." — Evangelist HAROLD D. COOMER

"*Delivered* is a heartwrenching love story, an incredible testimony to the power of God, and an inspiring book of hope for individuals seeking release from the bondage of addiction."
— SARAH HARKLESS, founder of Olivia's House

"Janet Gillispie shares her story in a way that causes our jaws to drop at the sorts of transformations that only Jesus can make possible for those willing to confess their sin and turn to God."
— REV. DOUG DORTCH, senior minister, Mountain Brook Baptist Church

"A beautiful picture of God's redeeming love and restoring power."
— CANDACE MCINTOSH, executive director, Alabama WMU

Brittany

What a joy to meet you and to see your shine of Jesus. May God lead you in love. Janet

DELIVERED

A MEMOIR

My Dark Path Through Addiction

JANET GILLISPIE WITH SAMMIE JO BARSTOW

NEW HOPE
PUBLISHERS
Gospel-Centered. Missions-Driven.

BIRMINGHAM, ALABAMA

New Hope® Publishers
P. O. Box 12065
Birmingham, AL 35202-2065
NewHopeDigital.com
New Hope Publishers is a division of WMU®.

Library of Congress Cataloging-in-Publication Data
Gillispie, Janet.
  Delivered, a memoir : my dark path through addiction / Janet Gillispie with Sammie Jo Barstow.
     pages cm
  ISBN 978-1-59669-377-7 (sc)
  1. Gillispie, Janet. 2. Christian converts--Alabama--Birmingham--Biography.
3. Alcoholism--Religious aspects--Christianity. 4. Substance abuse--Religious aspects--Christianity. 5. Prostitution--Religious aspects--Christianity. I. Barstow, Sammie Jo. II. Title.
  BV4935.G55A3 2013
  248.8'629092--dc23
  [B]

                              2012051767

Note: This is a true account, however, some names have been changed to protect the innocent.

Cover Design: Rare Design
Interior Design: Glynese Northam

ISBN-10: 1-59669-377-0
ISBN-13: 978-1-59669-377-7

N134118 • 0513 • 2M1

TABLE OF CONTENTS

DEDICATION

I would like to dedicate this story of God's redemption to Him who made the life I live today possible by death on the Cross for me. To my mother, Barbara Bernice Crampton, who is with the Lord now in that mansion. My mother loved me through all the dark years, never gave up on praying for me, and allowed her faith to grow even deeper for the Lord. What a blessing my mother was to me.

To my children, David, Steven Douglas, Brandon Lee, and Brittany Anne. I love you and thank God for giving to me His love, forgiveness, and grace so that I could finally love myself and so love you.

To a very special angel on earth, June Whitlow. You are Brittany's grandmother and like a mother to me. Our lives are beyond blessed because of your love for us. And to your best friend Pat Ferguson who is now Brittany's aunt.

I would also like to dedicate this story to you, the readers, who will allow your faith to grow deeper or for the first time. Just believe God is real.

To all those who have played a part in my new life in Christ.

ACKNOWLEDGMENTS

Wow! A new life, a new start, another chance, and for all my sins to be forgiven and forgotten! Saying thank you or making a list of acknowledgments does not seem to say or even penetrate what I hold in my heart and mind each and every day that I am able to live free. Going to work, getting my daughter ready for school, calling June on the way, and so much more than I could have ever imagined. To live in the joy, peace, and love of Christ that I am able to give and show to others, thank you. It is a word that could never contain how I feel about so many people and places who have played a part in the life I am able to live today and who I am today. I hope you all know how you are in me and a part of me forever and I love you all.

God, His Son Jesus Christ, and Holy Spirit for grace,
mercy, and deliverance

Barbara B. and Jerry M. Crampton, my mom and my dad

My children, especially Brittany

My brother, Stan Crampton

June Whitlow and Pat Ferguson, my family from God

The Gillispies

Ted Pearson and family

Dr. Richard Trucks and Third Presbyterian Church family

Dr. Harold and Susan Simon

Kathy Campbell

CJ Peach

Charlene Evans

Vicki Lyons

Olivia's House, Mrs. Sarah Harkless, founder

Yvas Witherspoon, my counselor

Alcoholics Anonymous, Mr. Ollie Ray and Kenneth Harkless

Narcotics Anonymous

Mountain Brook Baptist Church family

Pathways, Deisha Rosser

Christian Women's Job Corps, Dellanna O'Brien, founder

Catholic Family Services

Hannah Home, Odenville

Grace and Truth Church, Charles Mozley, my aftercare counselor

Glen Iris Baptist Church

First Baptist Church of Irondale

Childcare Resources

University of Alabama at Birmingham Early Head Start

My co-workers Christy, Amanda, Casondra, Caron, and John

The staff of the radiology and operating room at UAB Hospital, who have always encouraged me and helped me with donations and gifts for all the great causes I get involved with.

United Way of Central Alabama

WMU

The many churches who have welcomed me and allowed God's story of redemption and deliverance to be told

Sammie Barstow, for helping me tell this true story

Especially New Hope Publishers for letting God's story be told to the world

Thank you all for forgiveness and understanding and extending the love of Christ to me.

Janet Gillispie

How great is our God! I find myself in awe that He brought Janet into my life and that He has allowed us to tell this story together. I knew when I met Janet that God was already using her to speak to women in churches, classes, and civic groups, but I also sensed that He wanted this incredible story of redemption and transformation to have a larger audience. I'm so grateful that I could be part of helping that to happen.

As is true with any book, a writer is not alone in the process. My list of encouragers would fill a book by itself!

God blessed me with the two most incredible daughters! They have both believed in the project from the start, and their love and support has been beyond precious to me. Thank you, Lori White and Leslie Sulenski. I love you so much! Love also to: Matt, Dani, and Nicholas; Eric, Michael, and Mavinee; Ben and Linda; Chad, Mary, and Jalen; Leah, Wadie, and Laynie.

My local writers group, Tuscaloosa Christian Freelance Writers Club, has been in my corner all the way. Joanne and David Sloan and Cheryl Sloan Wray have mentored me through the learning-to-write-and-publish process for many years. I'm still learning and they're still teaching!

For the past ten years, my life has been so enriched by the Book Snobs, my book club. Lori, Pat, Celeste, Diana, Debra, Leigh, Janice, Annelle, Beth, and Anne Margaret—y'all are the greatest! Life would be a blank book without you!

Lisa Estes Ford and Judy Woodward Bates read the early manuscript and gave me invaluable help. I love, love, love them both for being my friends and for all those red marks on my manuscript! Also, my good friend and writer, Peggy Darty, who is now at home with the Lord, was a constant encourager and adviser. From the moment Rosalie Hunt heard about this project, she inspired me to believe that this book would become a reality, and I am so thankful for that.

I am blessed with many friends who regularly asked, "What about the book?" To all of you, I appreciate your overwhelming support.

At the point where Janet had told me her complete story and the writing was beginning, my dear friends Jean and Joe Powell provided me with a month of quiet, focused writing time by letting me stay in their beach condo. What a precious gift! Thank you, thank you!

Andrea Mullins, Joyce Dinkins, Tina Atchenson, and all the fabulous folks at New Hope Publishers — thank you for loving this project as much as Janet and I do. We appreciate you!

More than anything else, I'm thankful for the message of salvation that God gives through Janet's testimony. A new beginning is possible for every person who believes.

> "I have been crucified with Christ and I no longer live, but Christ lives in me. The life I live in the body, I live by faith in the Son of God, who loved me and gave himself for me" (Galatians 2:20 NIV).

To God be the glory!

Sammie Jo Barstow

INTRODUCTION

Sirens screamed through the air that day — November 11, 2000. I knew they were coming for me . . . and I was furious. Slowly regaining consciousness, I realized I was lying in the dry fall grass in Phelan Park where I had collapsed a few minutes earlier. I squinted into the sun as my wino buddies stared down at me. Another contraction raged through my abdomen. This baby was coming soon, but I had determined months ago that the birth of my fourth child would be nothing more than a temporary inconvenience.

Another hit. Please, just one more hit before they take me away. One more hit.

Through the previous night when my labor began and into the morning and early afternoon, I had fought against the inevitable. Now, lying in the grass and knowing the ambulance was seconds away, I had no choice.

I felt the strong arms of the EMTs lifting me onto the gurney and into the ambulance. I couldn't physically fight back, but I screamed and cursed and ranted. I called them every nasty name I could think of.

"Hold on, ma'am. Just a few more minutes and we'll be at the hospital."

I saw their smirks and eye rolls, and I felt their disgust. Yes, I was filthy, smelly, and despicable. I had on the same clothes I'd worn for months, and I hadn't taken a bath or brushed what few teeth I still had for at least two weeks. I had turned one trick for $5 and begged $3 off the guy who was filling the newspaper stand to get the $8 that bought my last hit.

And now — I was about to have a baby.

The ambulance screeched to a stop at the emergency entrance and the race was on.

"Move it! Move it! She's delivering!"

Out of the ambulance, rushing at breakneck speed for the delivery room. Pure chaos. Everyone yelling. I was cursing and screaming at the top of my lungs.

I could feel the baby's head pushing down hard.

"Get it out! Get it out of me! Get this thing out of me and let me go! You can't make me stay here!"

All I wanted was to get it over with and get back to the drug house. If I could just get there, surely somebody would feel sorry for me and give me a hit.

"Get it out!"

And then it happened.

The next few minutes changed my life forever.

Chapter 1

SEARCHING FOR LOVE

I didn't get to be an alcoholic, drug-addicted prostitute by one poor decision or one unfortunate circumstance, of course. My journey into the darkest life imaginable developed over many years. But once begun, every day was one more slippery slide into a pit so deep and so tortured that I couldn't climb out by my own strength.

I could easily blame my mistakes on other people. My parents who didn't show me affection. A boy who tempted me with sweet words of love. The parade of men who held me and told me what I wanted to hear—and then left. The drug dealer who taught me to trade my body for the best price. Or maybe the dealers who supplied my need and then threw me out when I'd spent my last dollar.

But laying blame on someone else isn't what it's all about for me now. My future is bright and full of love, but it's a different kind of love than I even knew existed until 12 years ago.

My story really begins the summer after seventh grade in Birmingham, Alabama. I was happier than I could ever imagine. Although my own family was dysfunctional, I met and fell in love with another family, and a young boy held me close and told me I was beautiful. I craved that kind of affection and love.

Toward the end of that school year, one of my teachers, Miss Cameron, began showing me special attention. She was a young, pretty, black woman who was divorced and had a son, Pete. She often let me help grade papers and do things for her after school, and then she'd take me home. On the last day of school, she invited me to go home with her for her son's fifth birthday party. I was thrilled to be with my favorite teacher.

Miss Cameron and Pete lived with her parents and her younger sister. It was a warm spring day, and their backyard was full of people laughing and talking. Several tables were set up with birthday tablecloths, decorations, and the most delicious food I'd ever eaten. The birthday boy and about a dozen other kids were running around the yard, having a great time.

I was the only white girl there, but it didn't seem to matter to anyone. It certainly didn't matter to me. But this was Birmingham in 1972, and Blacks and Whites still didn't socialize much. I'd never been raised to think I shouldn't have black friends. The truth was, I really didn't have *any* friends, black or white. But that was about to change.

During the party, a young boy drove up in a white pickup filled with watermelons. I guess my white skin and long blonde hair made me easy to spot. He got out of his truck and strutted over to me. Don was full of confidence, medium height and frame, with beautiful brown skin, a short Afro and a little gap between his two front teeth. When he smiled, I thought he was the cutest guy I'd ever seen.

Don and I talked for a long time. I was pretty shy, and my only real contact with boys was when my brother's friends came by our house. Sometimes I'd play football or ride bikes with them, but this kind of talking was something new and different for me. I could tell Don liked me.

Even on that first night, Don stirred up feelings in me I'd never experienced. Like somebody cared. Like I mattered to somebody. His whole family seemed to really like me. When I was supposed to go home, Miss Cameron asked me if I'd like to stay. I think she thought it was cute that Don and I hit it off so quickly. Miss Cameron called my mom and she agreed that I could stay overnight.

Things at my house weren't all that great. My mom and dad were good people, but there were many problems in my family. Dad had retired from the army and worked the night shift as a USDA inspector at the local poultry plant. He provided the living and Mom never worked outside the house. When he came home in the morning, he'd usually drink a while, sleep, and go back to work.

Dad was an alcoholic, but I didn't even know that word back then. I just knew Mom stayed upset with him a lot and that he didn't know much about what went on with my brother, Stan, and me. He was either at work, passed out, or on the way to being passed out.

That whole summer was a wonderful escape from my normal life. Spending time with Miss Cameron and Don's family was like finding the family I never had and the affection and happy feelings that I wanted so much. Don was 15 and one of six children. His parents overwhelmed me with kindness.

Don's mother and all the other women in that neighborhood were outstanding cooks. Caramel cake, chocolate pie, fried chicken, mounds of mashed potatoes. It was soul food and my hungry soul needed it. I thrived on the food and the love.

Miss Cameron and Don both had lots of kinfolks and they were all close. Everybody knew everybody else in their small neighborhood. Their houses were continually full of people and plenty of laughter, good food, and happiness. I never had experienced any of this and I thought I surely was in heaven. I quickly decided that this was the kind of happy family I wanted when I married and had children.

Don and I continued to get to know each other over the summer. We'd sit for hours on his front porch and talk, or we'd watch television in Miss Cameron's living room. We walked all over the community, holding hands and talking. I fell in love that summer.

Don would hold me and tell me how much he loved me. He told me I was beautiful. Kisses and hugs, nothing more than that. I don't know if I even knew anything more would happen. I was just incredibly happy.

Growing up in a small family — just my parents, my brother, and me — we didn't have much contact with uncles, aunts, cousins, or grandparents. We never had parties or family gatherings with food and people laughing and joking.

Don's family was completely different. Always so many people around, so much noise and excitement. So much love. That was it, really. So much love. I was just enveloped in their love and happiness.

But summer came to an end. Being back in school meant less time with Don, but he called every night, and we talked for hours. Sometimes Don and I would fall asleep talking on the phone.

Don was the man of my dreams. I felt that the fairy-tale life of "happily ever after" was right around the corner.

I did well in school, but Don was always in trouble, getting suspended for one thing or another, playing hooky and getting caught at it. But one thing about Don was that he always worked hard. He had a job at a local hamburger place, but he also helped his father sell watermelons and did all kinds of extra jobs. He saved his money and bought a little clunker of a car, so when he got his driver's license he was able to come to my house.

Don being black didn't seem to matter to my mother. He'd come over once or twice a week and Mother liked him. My brother usually kept to himself and didn't say much one way or the other. Of course, we lived in a White neighborhood and I'm sure there was some talk.

My father was another story. Many times when Don visited, my father was passed out and didn't even know he'd been there. When it finally dawned on him that Don was more than a friend, he told me we couldn't be together any more.

"What are you thinking, being with a black boy? What are all the neighbors thinking? Get rid of him, Janet." I told Mother we loved each other and wanted to be together. So Mother let Don come over when Daddy didn't know it, or she sometimes took me to see him. Since Don had a car and a driver's license, Mom would take me to meet him somewhere and we would ride around together.

I didn't care what other people said because no one had ever cared for me like this. Don filled a deep need, and I didn't want to lose that.

But I lived in a small community, and people did start talking. "Janet's seeing a black guy!" The other girls whispered about me in school and wouldn't sit with me at lunch. I noticed but didn't care one bit. I was riding a cloud to heaven. I had a boyfriend who loved me and showed me his love by the way he touched me and looked at me. All I could think about was how wonderful he made me feel.

In those first few months of dating Don, he introduced me to a lot of new experiences. I'd never been to a concert, but Don took me and my brother to a ball park called Rickwood Field in Birmingham to see Rare Earth, the Staple Singers, B. B. King, and Sly and the Family Stone.

I remember smelling a weird odor and seeing people acting goofy and happy. Don said they were smoking marijuana. The concert was in an open field, and people were passing marijuana cigarettes all around. I got a little high just being in the area, but then someone offered me a drag. Don said it was OK. *What a feeling!* I thought.

As Don and I got closer and I met some of his friends, I found out that they pretty much all liked their "weed." Being with friends meant a little wine and a little weed. It was fun, and I thought it was pretty harmless. After all, Don loved me, and I trusted that he wouldn't let anything happen that would hurt me. He was my protector, my knight in shining armor, my prince.

I fell harder and harder for Don. I wanted to be with him all the time. I wanted his arms around me. I wanted his kisses and his loving touches. You can imagine what happened next.

Don had a friend who lived in a mobile home. One night after we'd been drinking wine and smoking pot, Don took me there. We went into the middle bedroom and lay down on the bed. Don was sweet and loving. His touch was tender, and the pleasure and passion I felt was intense. I gave myself to him completely. I remember crying afterward because of the discomfort, but I also remember Don holding me and telling me it was all right, telling me how much he loved me. He said we'd get married and be together like this forever. I believed every word of it. I wanted nothing more than to belong to Don and be loved by him.

After that night, almost every time we were together it was the same. I don't think my mother knew. We didn't talk about those kinds of things. She would have been embarrassed and I would, too, so we just didn't.

My mother had warned me about letting men touch me when I was a little girl, but we didn't talk about what happens between a boy and girl in love. She sure didn't talk with me about saving myself for marriage or the possibility of getting pregnant. I think she just saw this relationship with Don as a sweet thing between two young kids.

As Don and I spent more time together and showed our affection in public by holding hands, hugging, and all that, people made racial remarks about us. Our families were more concerned now too. My dad was pretty angry about it, so we more or less hid from him. Don's mother and grandmother were worried. They didn't want anything to happen to either one of us. But my mom liked Don, and his family continued to love me, so no one tried to break us up.

Christmas that year with Don's family was stunning. Lights, food, family, happiness, love. Presents under the tree and spilling out all over the living room. I couldn't wait until Don and I could get married and have a home of our own. I vowed to make our home just like his family's, filled with laughter and love.

By now, Don and I were really serious and everybody knew it. We were talking about when we could get married and, in the meantime, we were drinking and dabbling in drugs. Mostly we smoked pot, but occasionally we'd try a block of acid or a pill of some kind. One time somebody had a jug of moonshine and we even tried that. The drinking and drugs got heavier and more frequent. Almost every time we were together, we were getting drunk or high. And being intimate.

Both of us were searching for something and we thought we'd found it in each other. The booze and the drugs just made everything better. Or so we thought.

I don't have any idea why I didn't get pregnant because I never used birth control. I didn't know what that was or how to get it. That was a long time before teenagers were able to walk into a counseling center or clinic and get birth control pills without parental consent.

Don was thinking about our future, and he decided to join the army. He had dropped out of school, so job possibilities were not good. I completely supported his plan. Don would join the army, go through basic training, and be stationed somewhere. We'd get married, and I'd join him. Just the thought made me deliriously happy.

While Don was in the army, I lived mostly with his parents, Annie and Robert. They treated me like a daughter, and I loved them too. Annie was a large woman with a sweet smile and an even sweeter heart. She was quiet, but Robert was more outgoing. He was tall and thin and loved to talk and have fun. They both seemed lighthearted and happy.

Don's brother, Greg, still lived at home and he was a party boy. We hit it off. Greg was a wild comedian. He could always make me laugh. Since I wasn't in school, I had lots of time on my hands. Greg and I would go shoot pool and drink a little. After all, he was almost my brother-in-law, I thought. Sometimes we'd drink too much and when we came in, Don's mother, Annie, would say, "Now, y'all better watch yourselves." But we kept on hanging out, getting drunk, shooting pool, and smoking marijuana together.

When Don called me, I would tell him how much I loved him and couldn't wait for him to come home. But lots of other guys were close by, and I wanted someone to hold me and say sweet things to me. I knew I was doing the wrong thing by flirting with other guys while my fiancé was away, but I didn't want the good feelings to stop. I stuffed those feelings of wrongdoing deep inside and refused to feel guilty.

I went to Fort Knox with Don's parents for his Advanced Individual Training graduation. My heart overflowed with pride and love for him. During that weekend, he gave me an engagement ring with a little diamond in it. I found out later he had bought it at a pawn shop, but that didn't matter to me. Of course, I accepted it and came home floating on a cloud.

I think Don's parents were happy for us, but I know they were concerned. They saw all the problems we would face as a mixed couple, but all I saw was excitement and love. When I got home, I told my mom I was engaged and would be married soon. She seemed OK with that. Mom wanted me to finish school but she didn't pressure me.

My father ranted furiously. I finally told him that I loved Don and I was going to marry him.

"I won't permit it, Janet!"

"You can't stop me! If you try, I'll run away!"

My dad cried. I'd never seen him cry! It wasn't that I hadn't seen him unhappy. That happened a lot. He was an unhappy man. I used to hear him say that he wanted to die. "Lord, just let me die," he'd say. I think there were a lot of emotions going around inside him. He couldn't control his drinking. He probably felt like a failure as a husband and a father, inadequate and insecure. Although I detested my father's drinking, I also felt sorry for him.

So when Don returned from basic training, Dad went to the courthouse with us and signed the papers giving permission for me to get married. I was 15 and Don was 17. I know Daddy was devastated, but I remember him saying, "Janet, I just want you to be happy." We found someone at the courthouse to marry us.

Don had sold his car when he went in the army and Annie bought us a used Mach 1 Mustang as a wedding gift. Don had already found us an off-base apartment at Fort Benning, Georgia, where he was stationed. Some of his relatives gave us a few pieces of furniture, and we moved in the apartment. I had everything I'd ever wanted. I had a husband who loved me and a place of my own.

Happy was my middle name.

Chapter 2

DEATH, BETRAYAL, AND HEARTBREAK

I loved everything about being a wife. I polished Don's boots and ironed his fatigues. I was so proud of him. Even learning to cook was fun. I'd never cooked with my mother, so I didn't know anything about it. Mom was very organized and neat. Sometimes she was a perfectionist in what she did and what she expected of me. She wouldn't have been able to put up with mistakes. I knew I'd never do it right in her eyes, so I just didn't try. Now I learned on my own and delighted in preparing wonderful meals for Don, learning a new recipe almost every night.

Living in our little apartment complex was great fun. The wives spent time together during the days, talking, doing our nails, sharing our lives, and waiting for our husbands to come home in the evenings. Our apartment was tiny and our possessions were minimal, but I delighted in keeping everything spotless and using the washer and dryer at the end of the complex to do our laundry. How could life be any happier?

I found my Prince Charming. We would start our family soon and I'd have that closeness and bonding that my family never had. Don's family had shown me what it would be like to have a happy family, and I knew we'd have the same thing with our children.

Don and I were married on January 3, 1975, and by February I was pregnant. I was ecstatic and Don was too. I couldn't wait to tell everyone at home. As soon as I realized I was pregnant, I made plans for a weekend trip home to share the news.

On a weekend when Don was gone on maneuvers, I took a Greyhound bus to Birmingham. When I got home, my dad wasn't feeling well. Mom talked him into going to their family doctor. He soon returned home saying the doctor wanted him to go to the hospital for some tests, but he wanted Mom to take him to Fort McClellan Army Hospital in Anniston, Alabama, about 70 miles from Birmingham. Daddy was retired military, and we had been stationed at Fort McClellan when Stan and I were children.

I realize now that Daddy wasn't letting us know how sick he was. Because of his alcoholism, he suffered from pancreatitis as well as heart problems. He was only 56, but his health had deteriorated so much that he looked much older. My dad had black hair and brown eyes, much different from my mother with her blonde hair and fair skin. Dad always looked like he had a tan, but that was his natural coloring. Now he looked pale and sickly.

When I was younger, he was always pretty stout, but the alcohol had caused health issues that brought on weight loss. By the time we made this trip to Fort McClellan he was thin and unhealthy looking. During that drive to the hospital, Daddy sat in the backseat and stared out the window, looking so sad and hopeless.

I felt like I never knew my dad, and we never really expressed love to each other, but I do know he loved me. His way of showing love was to earn a living. He went to work every day and provided what the family needed even when his drinking was at its worst. He handed Mom his paycheck and she managed the household. That was his way of loving us. I know he did his best to be a good father, but the alcohol choked out everything else in his life.

My heart breaks when I think about how many feelings he must have had locked up inside. The only way he seemed to know how to deal with them was by popping open another bottle.

When we got to Fort McClellan hospital, they took my dad for testing, and we didn't get to see him until that afternoon. He was lying on a bed, unresponsive, and attached to all kinds of monitors. Mom burst into tears when she saw him. I didn't know what to think.

Moments later, Daddy coded. The medical people pushed us aside and worked furiously to save him. They couldn't. Within minutes, he was dead. It just didn't seem possible. We had left home that morning thinking he was going to have some tests, and, just a few short hours later, he was dead. I had gone home to tell my parents they would soon be grandparents, and he died within hours of hearing the happy news.

The next few days were a blur. There was no burial because my dad had made arrangements for his body to be donated to science. The shock of what had happened was overwhelming. My heart was so empty. I knew my mother needed me to stay, but all I wanted was to get back to my husband and our little apartment. I wanted him to hold me and take away the pain. I thought if I could get back home to Don, maybe this horrible grief would lift.

Mother agreed for me to leave and drove me to the bus station. Don didn't know I was coming, so I took a cab from the bus station to our apartment. I couldn't wait to see him and feel his arms around me. I knew he'd make it all better. But I was in for the surprise of my young life.

I walked into our apartment to find Don in bed with a woman. Needless to say, I was shocked. I thought I was going to faint, so I collapsed on the couch, sobbing hysterically. The woman jumped up, threw on her clothes, and raced by me and out the door.

Don sat down and tried to pull me into his arms. He was mumbling some lame explanation, but I wasn't listening. I turned around and starting beating his chest with my fists. Happily ever after was gone. Here I was, 15 years old, married, pregnant, my father had just died, and my husband was with another woman. It was more than I could comprehend.

All those conversations Don and I had had about our beautiful future together flashed through my mind. My vision of a happy marriage, loving family, even the sparkling Christmases I longed for—the whole picture shattered into a million pieces in just a few seconds.

I called my mother and told her I wanted to come home. I sobbed my heart out to her. I called Don's mother and she said,

"Work through it, Janet. Men do things like this. It will be all right." I knew it would never be all right again. I just wanted to go home. I felt like a little girl.

Mother said I could come home, so I picked up my suitcase, which I hadn't even opened, and took a cab right back to the Greyhound bus station. In a few hours, I was on a bus headed back to Birmingham. I thought of my daddy and how he gazed out the car window on the way to the hospital. My face must have mirrored the same hopelessness I saw in his face that day.

I received plenty of advice in those next few weeks. One of my mother's friends said, "You're pregnant with a black man's baby. You'll never be accepted and neither will that baby. No white man will want you now. Just go and have an abortion and start your life over. You're only 15. It's not too late."

But I didn't look at it that way. All I could think of was how my happiness bubble had burst wide open. My fairy-tale life was in ruins. The pain, hurt, and deceit weighed heavy on my heart, but I knew I couldn't kill my baby. That would only add to all this suffering.

In my immaturity, I really thought I was going to have a cuddly little baby who would coo and grin and make me OK again. Surely a baby would fill all my needs for love and affection. I certainly didn't consider any of the responsibility of raising a child alone.

Don came to Birmingham several times to try to persuade me to come back, but I just couldn't do it. I still loved him, but I knew that I couldn't trust him. I heard someone say that trust is like a piece of paper. After being crumpled, it never is completely perfect again. This was the first of many, many betrayals I would experience in the next 30 years.

Chapter 3

A PARENT, BUT STILL A CHILD

I spent my days at Mom's house watching TV, eating, and feeling sorry for myself. On October 9, 1975, I gave birth to a beautiful baby boy, David Gerard Gillispie. I was a pretty good mother at first, I think. Here was this sweet little baby I could hold and love and care for. I wanted him to fill all the empty spaces in my heart. Did those feelings last? Of course not. The reality of daily life with a baby, loss of sleep, and the weight of responsibility all began to overpower me.

I got a small allotment check from the army for a couple of years until our divorce was final. Don's parents provided diapers and baby clothes and did all they could to help me, so for a while I was cared for financially.

Even though I had a child, I was still a child myself in spite of all I had already experienced. I still wanted to be held by a man who loved me, to feel complete and satisfied in my heart. I thought that longing for completeness could only be filled by having a new boyfriend and hearing him declare his love for me, so I clung to the rare moments when I found those feelings. Usually those times also meant drinking, and smoking marijuana, or an occasional hit of acid.

I was sliding farther down the slope into the kind of life that promised pleasure and good feelings but, instead, always ended in hopelessness and desperation. Drugs, alcohol, the next party, the next new boyfriend. That's all I thought about.

It was a difficult time for my mother too. Stan was still in high school and at home. She was dealing with the grief of my father's death, and now she had a daughter and a grandbaby to add to that stress. She faced loss of income and insecurity about her future too. Taking care of David was some diversion, but I forced her to take on far too much responsibility for him. I wanted to be out and gone rather than home taking care of a crying baby.

Mom was getting tired of me hanging around the house with no purpose. I was eating too much and watching TV or sleeping while she took care of David. Of course, I had little potential for getting a job or making any money since I hadn't even graduated high school. Who would hire me?

Mom suggested that I take the GED test at a local community college. I made a good score, so they offered me a grant to start school there. I wasn't particularly excited about that, but what else was I going to do? Also, I figured it would get me away from home, away from my responsibilities with David. Maybe I'd meet some new people. Don had the car Annie had given us as a wedding present. To encourage me and help me get started in school, Annie and Robert bought me a used blue Chevy Nova.

When I enrolled at Jefferson State Community College, I had no idea what I'd study. I was kind of interested in the medical fields, so I took a chemistry class the first semester thinking I might try nursing. I didn't have the background I needed for that and almost failed the class. I also took a couple of secretarial courses, but I knew I couldn't spend all day behind a desk.

I got a part-time job at the chicken plant where my father had been a USDA inspector, so I was working, going to school, trying to be a mother, and hanging out with friends. My mother was taking on more and more of the responsibility for David, and Annie frequently took him to her house for days at a time.

Even after working and school, I still spent most of my nights staying out late, drinking, doing drugs, and partying. It was a juggling act. I knew I wasn't being a good mother, but I was trying to mix my responsibilities as a parent with the yearnings of a 17-year-old girl's heart for belonging, fitting in, and just plain having fun.

After working at the chicken plant a few months, I got a job at a company that makes fire extinguishers, and met a new guy,

Mack, a forklift operator. He was about five years older than me and had long, coal-black hair and a big, thick beard. He loved to play guitar and I could spend hours just listening to his music and feeling like I was in another world.

I thought Mack was the hippie-est person I'd ever met, except that he was a better dresser than most hippies I knew. And he told me I had "a fine butt." Excuse me, but that's what he said. Him hitting on me by telling me I was "pretty and fine" was all it took for me to believe he cared for me. Nice words that made me feel good about myself again.

Mack and I would work the 3:00 to 11:00 shift and then go to his place and do a pill or smoke marijuana and hang out together. In the early morning hours, I'd go home and climb in bed with my little boy. Mother would fuss at me. "Why can't you stay home? I'm not going to be the mother to this child."

But I'd talk her into it. "It's Friday night and I've worked hard all week. Please let me go out."

I thought Mack cared for me, and I was falling hard for him too. He rented a room in a large house owned by a friend, but the other guy was seldom there. We'd usually have the whole house to ourselves. Sometimes other people would come over and we'd sit around and drink and do our drugs. Mack would play the guitar, and it all felt so cool.

One night Mack and I and another couple were at a friend's apartment doing the usual things. Mack and I went in a bedroom while the other couple went in another room. Then Mack said, "OK, now let's swap."

I had no idea what he was talking about.

"I'll go in and be with his girl and he'll come in here and be with you," he said.

I'd never even heard of such a thing. He tried to persuade me that this is just something people do for fun. "It doesn't mean anything, Janet. It's just for fun." I burst into tears, ran out of the apartment, jumped in my little Chevy, and left. We never dated after that.

Heartbroken again. *What is wrong with me?* How could Mack love me and feel like it was OK for another man to have me?

By then, I was 18, working at night, going to school, trying to be a mom, lonely and miserable. I felt guilty about how I was treating David. Many times I'd go off on the weekend or leave for work or school and my little boy would cry and reach for me. But I would push those feelings of guilt out of my mind and tell myself I couldn't let that hurt me.

He's got Mom and Annie. They love him. They take care of him better than I do. I didn't love him like I should because I was still looking for love myself. I know that's wrong, but I was immature and thinking only about myself.

I had thought a baby would make me feel loved; but, of course, it wasn't what I expected. I thought I'd have all the precious, sweet times that come with having a baby, but I hadn't counted on the difficult times. Now I realize how ridiculous that was.

Searching. Always searching.

Chapter 4

A DOWNHILL DECADE

I had always been a little chubby and, of course, after having the baby I had gained some weight. I'd flirt with my brother's friends and guys at school and then look at myself and think maybe I was too fat and that's why they didn't want me.

I really don't remember exactly how this began, but I had heard about some girls who would eat and then make themselves throw up to lose the weight, so I started doing that. This quickly got out of hand. I'd end up eating twice as much as usual and then throw it up. That way I could stuff myself to the point of being totally uncomfortable and then get rid of it. Of course, no one knew what I was doing.

After purging, I would feel sleepy and relaxed. I later learned that bingeing and purging releases endorphins and stimulants in the same kind of euphoria as crack cocaine. Many days when I left school or work I'd go buy three large hamburgers, a couple of orders of fries, and a shake, and I'd eat it all. Then I'd go home and throw it up. So now my days were full of school, work, pot-smoking, drinking, bingeing, and purging.

My mother started getting suspicious. She would stand outside the bathroom door and hear me vomiting. Neither she nor I knew to use the term *bulimia* or that what I was doing was a medical disorder, but she was concerned. It made me angry for her to talk to me about it. Just another indication, I thought, that she didn't really love me.

Bingeing and purging became a daily occurrence, sometimes more than once a day. I wanted so much to be beautiful, and

I thought if I lost weight and stayed skinny I would be prettier and more attractive to someone. But men came and went. A few drinks, some weed, and a night or two together—and they were gone.

I figured nothing else made a man love me enough to stay with me, so it had to be my looks. I'd fix that. When I looked in the mirror, I saw a fat girl even though I got down to 85 pounds. At 5 feet 6 inches tall, I was painfully thin, but all I could think of was that if I lost a little more weight maybe I'd be more attractive to someone. I had the little pot belly that goes along with bulimia and malnutrition.

I got involved with one of my brother's friends, Dean. Oh, he was fine! Dean had long, blondish-gold hair and big muscles. He was a football player in high school and I knew him from a distance and had a crush on him even back then. He was also a party boy, beer drinker, and pot smoker. My kind of guy. I fell for him and gave in to him. He liked his women thin, so staying that way became more important. Dean was a popular guy with a good sense of humor. Everybody liked him, so I thought if I was Dean's girl, everyone would like me too. People would say, *Wow, she's got Dean. She must be something special!*

My son was four years old, and I rarely saw him. Mom and Annie took care of him. I know he missed his mama, but, sad to say, that wasn't important to me. When I began feeling guilty about David, I shoved those thoughts right out of my mind. I was 19 and all I wanted to do was party.

My brother and his girlfriend had gotten an apartment and they had an extra bedroom, so that made it great for Dean and me. We'd have a lot of people over, smoke pot, get drunk, do a little acid or angel dust, and listen to rock music. Then we'd go to my brother's extra bedroom. Dean said he loved me, and I thought, once more, that I had everything I wanted. I was still going to school and had decided to be a radiological technologist. I had a little more focus, but studying still wasn't a high priority.

Dean came up with the idea of moving to Texas because he thought we could get better jobs there. Two guys who were Dean's friends wanted to go with us. Dean said he would marry me and I could finish school in Texas as soon as we got settled in.

The four of us went to Houston, and we all got jobs. The guys worked in construction, and I got a job at a factory that canned soda. We'd ride to work together every day and stop on the way home to buy our beer or whiskey. We were able to get plenty of other drugs, too, so that's how we spent our time off work.

I soon discovered why Dean wanted me to come along with them. I ended up cooking every night, doing their laundry, and cleaning the apartment. All they wanted to do was drink, smoke pot, and pass out every night. Usually somebody peed on themselves and I'd clean that up too. Whenever I mentioned getting married, Dean changed the subject. Likewise for going back to school. It wasn't happening.

But I stuck it out about six months. Didn't call home much. Didn't even talk to my son but a couple of times. Mom and Annie passed him back and forth, a week or two at a time. I was so immature about caring for my son. I just wanted to be Dean's girl and to feel loved.

What I ended up feeling like was a maid and a mother to three grown men. Whatever I hoped for in Houston didn't turn out to be any different than what I'd had in Birmingham.

One day I was off work and the guys had left money for me to pay the rent. I took that money, got a cab to the airport, and bought a one-way ticket back to Birmingham. I asked my mother to take me in one more time. She did.

Of course, Dean and the other guys called me, yelling and cursing and saying I owed them money. I said, "Hey, I did what I had to do. You owed it to me for all the cooking, cleaning, and laundry I did for you."

When the next semester began, I returned to radiology school. Again, my mind wasn't on my studies, but school was a place to be. During the next year, I was still smoking pot on the way to class and going outside on breaks to take a puff or two. Still finding people who liked their pot and their drink. Still making all the same mistakes with guys.

I started working occasionally at a bar near my mother's house. Sometimes when I was there, I noticed an older man paying attention to me. He was a frequent customer, so I got to know him.

Chuck was rich and he treated me like a lady, something I'd really never experienced. He was 14 years older than me, and I liked that maturity. I guess some people would say I was looking for a father. He was a little plump, medium height, and had thinning hair which was short and curly. Certainly not the look I'd always fallen for before.

He took me to nice restaurants and gave me money to shop for clothes and jewelry. He dressed nicely and seemed to enjoy seeing me dressed up and fixed up. I never saw him except on weekends when we'd go out to eat or do something else and then go back to his place. I'd stay with Chuck on weekends, but during the week he traveled with his work.

When Chuck found out I had been married to a black man and had a son by him, he couldn't deal with that. He told me we could have a future together if I would give my son away. Although I wasn't concerned with taking care of David, and actually had given him away by not taking responsibility for him, I thought Chuck's attitude was heartless. We broke up then, but Chuck would be part of my life for years to come. I think he always loved me, and he certainly helped me through some extremely difficult times in my life.

It's pretty ironic that I was so offended by Chuck's attitude about David when I cared so little about being a mother to my little boy. When David was ready to start kindergarten, Annie approached me about adopting him. She said I could see him whenever I wanted, but she thought he would have a better life growing up in a Black community. To tell the truth, I was relieved. Now I knew David would have a stable life and I could go on doing all the things I'd put before him but without the guilt. At least, that's what I thought.

I completed my clinical training, finished the associate's degree in radiological technology, took the licensing test, and got a job at the hospital where I had done my training. I recently found a picture of a group of students taken when we finished school. No one would ever recognize me in that picture. I was pale and extremely thin. Still bingeing and purging.

Dean had moved back to Birmingham and I was still seeing him now and then. As I think back to all that I was doing back then, I think I might have been trying to fill the lonely places inside me with my behaviors. All that was really filling me was an enormous amount of guilt and shame, but I felt powerless to live any other way.

I worked at the first hospital for about a year and then got a job at a different hospital, working 7:00 P.M. to 7:00 A.M. in the emergency room. I had gotten a little efficiency apartment on the top floor of a ten-story apartment building on Highland Avenue in Birmingham. I had two hot plates and a refrigerator, and I washed dishes in the bathtub. A twin bed folded out from a closet in the wall.

My bingeing and purging by then was completely out of control. Sometimes when we didn't have much work during the night at the hospital, I'd go down to the snack bar and buy three cheeseburgers. They had the best cheeseburgers you'll ever eat. Then I'd go to the bathroom or a closet somewhere to eat them all and puke. Of course, at our regular lunch hour, I'd go eat again. People were always bringing food and leaving it in the ER. Sandwiches, cakes, cookies. I ate it all. Then I'd go to the bathroom and purge.

My routine was to leave the hospital at 7:00 A.M. and go home and make my own margaritas. I'd drink three or four of those, smoke some marijuana, and pass out. In the afternoon, I'd get up and go to buy several cheeseburgers, two or three fries, and a large shake. Then I'd stop at the grocery store and buy some chocolate chip cookies and maybe a gallon of ice cream. I'd go home, eat it all, and heave.

By then, my body was worn out, so I'd take a nap, wake up, smoke some more reefer, and go to work. I was destroying myself. But that was just the beginning.

I don't know how my body stood up to all the malnutrition, drugs, alcohol, and other abuse. One of my lowest points in those early years was having gall bladder surgery. Gallstones are a natural result of bingeing and purging, and I was so thin that it's a wonder I survived. I feared I wouldn't make it. I remember being in the hospital alone. Dean had disappeared. I had no one.

I called my mother, thinking I was going to die during the surgery. I told her I loved her and that I was sorry for all the things I'd put her through. I'd heard that the singer Karen Carpenter died as a result of bingeing and purging, and I thought that was about to happen to me.

Even though I recovered from that illness and surgery, things were going from bad to worse in many ways. I almost never saw my son or even talked to him. I didn't want to talk to Annie because I knew she was doing the job I should have been doing for my child. I didn't see my mother very much either. Every time I did, she would say I was too skinny and she guessed I was still puking. I didn't want to be reminded of any of that. I didn't want anybody to bug me about anything. *This is my life*, I thought, *and they can all just stay out of it.*

Dean was still around off and on. He'd come and spend a few days or a week with me and then he'd be gone again. Sometimes when I didn't have any marijuana, I'd call Dean and he'd always know where I could buy a bag. When he'd call or come around, the door was always open and so was my heart. I guess I figured as long as he spent some time with me, I had part of him.

But I also found plenty of other people to do drugs with and lots of new drugs to try. Sometimes we'd get powder cocaine and sometimes crank, a homemade substance a lot of truck drivers used. You would snort it and it kept you awake. I'd get $25 worth of crank and it would last all night. It burned my nose something awful, but got me high as a kite.

One morning I was driving to work at the hospital and I had taken a sleeping pill. It's a "downer" and I thought, you know, I needed a little relaxing because I had been smoking cocaine all night. I had taken the pill to edge it off. Well, as I was getting on the interstate I veered off and hit a light pole. It broke and came right down on the top of my car. It didn't knock me out, so I got out of the car and flagged down some help. Here I was in my medical scrubs, definitely under the influence of alcohol and other drugs, and the police would be there any minute.

I put on a show. You know, "Hey, I'm OK, but I'm late for work. Just get me a tow truck and get my car towed in and I'll go on to work and I'll be fine." The policeman let me go. As soon as he pulled away, I dug in my purse and popped another pill.

Drinking and drugging. Bingeing and purging. Making up excuses and lies. Avoiding facing any realities. I was on a roller coaster headed downhill, but I didn't know how to stop. Truth is, I didn't even *want* to stop. I didn't know when or where I would crash and didn't care. I felt I had no one in my life who loved me and any high I got by drinking, drugging, and purging was all that mattered.

I couldn't see that my drug use or bingeing was an addiction or that I was doing anything wrong. I was blinded to it all. I can't explain it, but at that time, I thought this was normal living.

That kind of life is expensive, so I ended up getting a part-time job at yet another hospital in addition to my regular job so I could have more money to support my drug use. I still had three or four days off work every two weeks, and I'd spend that entire time getting high with Dean or someone else. Still bingeing and purging.

Carla, my x-ray partner at my main job, and I would clock each other in when one of us was late or wanted to get away and smoke something. Somebody squealed on us and, of course, they asked us to resign.

Birmingham has plenty of hospitals, so I got another job with no problem. That was where I met an orderly named Leon, a black, middle-aged man with a short Afro hairstyle with a touch of gray. He snorted cocaine. I didn't know what rock cocaine was until then, but Leon was my introduction into that world. Crack was readily available in the projects and hot dope spots, and Leon knew all the right places to buy it.

When you're using or you live that kind of life, you pick up on who does the same thing. It's something you have in common. Maybe it's the language we use or whatever, but Leon figured out I did a little drugging and I knew he did too. We began to share a joint or two now and then.

Dean worked part-time laying carpet. Since I worked 3:00 P.M. to 11:00 P.M., often by the time I got home he would have been drinking and whatever else and was passed out. So I would frequently call Leon and say, "Hey, I've got a few dollars and my man's passed out drunk. Let's go get some crack." We would ride to the projects around Birmingham. Leon knew all the spots. He'd run in and get a crack rock and we'd ride around and smoke it in a pipe.

Dean really liked to shoot up cocaine powder. Many times, especially on weekends when I would work, I'd come home at midnight and there would be an apartment full of people shooting up and needles everywhere. I tried it a few times, but I really didn't like that as much as smoking. They would all swap needles or, if they didn't have but one needle, they'd all use it and just wash it out with water.

Sometimes I'd spend all my money before payday and I'd be so desperate. *Please, please, just give me another hit. I'll get paid next week and I'll bring it to you. Please, please.* My whole addiction now was for crack, and I really didn't even smoke marijuana much anymore. That didn't do it for me.

During this time, I did not even think that I was prostituting to get drugs; I told myself I was just getting what I needed.

I was sinking deeper into debt to support my addiction. I had to pay my drug bills before anything else because the drug dealers would hunt me down to get the money I owed them. They knew my paydays and they would demand payment. Sometimes there was nothing left for paying the utilities, so something was always getting cut off. Plus, I'd start the next pay period with no money and no dope. The cycle would begin again. Buying drugs on credit, settling up on payday, nothing left.

I was often late to work or called in to say that I couldn't come, and I got further behind in owing money to the drug dealers. I borrowed money from people at work and then disappeared for days at a time before coming back to work so I wouldn't have them badgering me about the money.

It seemed like no matter what wrong things I did, people still liked me and tried to work with me to help me keep my job. One time my boss and the department secretary came to my apartment to check on me when I'd been out of work several days. When I answered the door, I was completely stoned, but they held my job for me even after that.

Sometimes I'd have to pawn my car to the drug man when I couldn't come up with enough money to pay my debt. Then I'd have to walk or bum a ride to work or just not go. I was also writing bad checks all over town. This was before they had ways of knowing instantly whether your check is good. It would take a few days for a check to clear the bank, so I'd write checks just hoping I could beat them to the bank on payday. When I couldn't, that meant paying the amount of the check as well as a bad check fee. I was drowning in drug debts and bad check charges.

I bought a car, a 1982 Ford hatchback sports car, and established credit in my name, so pretty soon I was getting preapproved credit cards in the mail. I maxed out every credit card I received. In no time, I was thousands of dollars in debt and ended up filing for bankruptcy.

Birmingham was home, but I had burned such a trail that I dared not get picked up or questioned because with all the bad checks floating around, time in jail was a sure thing.

Perhaps it was time to leave Birmingham again.

Chapter 5

MARRIED IN MISSISSIPPI

Dean decided we should leave town. His mother lived in Mississippi, so he thought we could move there, at least for a while, get jobs and work where we didn't have all these drug debts and bad check charges. No one would find us in Mississippi, he said.

Dean's mother and stepfather, Jayne and Martin, encouraged us to come, and I had already quit my job at the hospital before they could fire me for all the unexcused absences. While employed 1986 to 1989, I had contributed to the state retirement system, so when I quit I filed a claim to withdraw that money. A check for a little more than $3,000 came the week before we planned to move.

Well, man alive, we lived high for that week! Did we pay any drug debts or pick up any bounced checks and pay the fee? No way! We bought our drugs and alcohol. We had people in the apartment all day and night and supplied the drugs for everyone. We ordered pizza whenever we wanted to and bought other food too.

We thought we had it made. We would buy eight bottles of liquor at a time and share with everybody. When you're high and on a roll, you don't think about anything in the future and you don't face any realities. *I've got my whiskey. I've got my drugs. I've got my lover. Life is good.*

Sometime during that week, my mother and brother came to our apartment. I looked outside and saw it was them and wouldn't open the door. The whole apartment was full of drugs, smelling like marijuana, bottles of whiskey and beer everywhere. When we didn't answer, they broke down the door.

My mother was screaming at me. "Do you know what you're doing? What is wrong with you? You haven't even seen your son. You're messing up your whole life!"

She screamed at Dean too. She blamed him. We had a big scene and I told them to leave and to stay out of my business. "I hate you both and I never want to see you again!"

We lived high on the hog for one week and then it was over and there we were, hungry and broke. Not even money for a cigarette. Looking for butts somebody had thrown out of a car.

We decided to get on a bus and leave for Hickory, Mississippi. Actually, Dean's stepfather drove a Greyhound bus and his route took him through Tuscaloosa, a city southwest of Birmingham, so he picked us up.

Jayne and Martin didn't know we had any problems with drugs or anything else. We told them we got laid off our jobs and had a run of bad luck. And that's what I told myself too. *Here we are in a new place. No one knows us. No one will hound us for bad checks or other debts here. We can start over. We'll act like we don't have any problems and they'll believe us.*

Part of starting over was that Dean and I got married in 1990, after ten years of an off-and-on relationship. Jayne and Martin let us live with them. Jayne bought me a pretty dress and went to the jewelry store and charged plain gold wedding bands for us. We had the wedding at their house. Things were looking up.

I got an x-ray tech job at a hospital in Union, Mississippi, and Dean did odd jobs. It was hard for him to find a regular job because Hickory is a one-stoplight, one-service station, country town and there wasn't much work. But we were OK living with his parents and settling into married life. One huge drawback, though, was that we weren't able to do any drugs because we were living with Jayne and Martin.

Dean not working and both of us not having our crack led to a lot of arguments. After a few months of living with Jayne and Martin, we rented a little house where we could do whatever we wanted. But Dean ended up working less and less and that made me furious.

Back then, in the country bars, you brought your own liquor, and that was the thing to do for entertainment. Get together, drink, shoot pool, and whoop it up. That's what Dean and I did on the weekend and sometimes during the week. Then I would get up and go to the hospital and, if he had a job that day, he would do that, or he might stay passed out in the bed all day.

A lot of people we met took pills. They'd take several pills and drink a few beers and everything would seem loose and cool and mellow. That's the way pills affected most people, but I was different. When I mixed the pills and beer, I became violent. I'd want to fight and be rowdy and act like I'm the toughest girl. I'd say things and do things and not remember any of it. I was also blacking out after combining pills and beer.

One of the people who always had a supply of pills was William, Dean's friend who worked at a local furniture factory. He was tall, wore thick, black-rimmed glasses, and pretty much looked like a nerd. He was from a wealthy family, and I don't know how he always had pills, but he did. He also was coming on to me. I'd work 3:00 P.M. to 11:00 P.M. at the hospital and William would call me or send me flowers at work. Again, it was someone to make me feel special.

It wasn't long until William and I were seeing each other. So I was a married woman committing adultery. Here was a man who told me I was beautiful, opened doors for me, said sweet things to me, and treated me like a lady. He told me he was so glad he met me because he knew I was the woman for him. I was the woman he had dreamed of meeting all his life. Even though William wasn't much to look at, I thought he was the most romantic man I'd ever known. For ten years I had chased Dean, but now William was courting me and I loved the attention.

Dean and I were fighting all the time, and it became brutal. I ended up with broken ribs and had to get treated in the ER at the hospital where I worked. He was always drunk when I came home, so I gave up on him.

After all, here was William who treated me like a queen and said he loved me. He fulfilled all my needs. I decided I would divorce Dean and marry William and live happily ever after. It was the same story. I'd been through this so many times. Someone made me feel loved and I fell for it. My craving for attention and affection was almost as great as my craving for drugs and alcohol. William was just one in a long line of men who said the right words and did the right things. And then left me.

When Dean roughed me up and I ended up in the ER, William took me from the hospital to his house and babied me and pampered me until my wounds healed, so I convinced myself that he loved me. I left Dean and stayed with William. I'm sure this was humiliating to Dean. You know, he brought a woman to his hometown, married her, and now she'd left him for someone else.

One good thing that happened while I was in Mississippi and working at the hospital was that my mother cashed my income tax refund check, which came after I moved. She used that money to go around to businesses and pay off my bad checks. Some of those places had called her trying to contact me. This was God's way of taking care of me so that when I wanted to move back to Birmingham I wouldn't have to go to jail because of all the check charges.

My mother didn't know everything about Dean and me, but she totally blamed Dean for all the bad things I was doing. I guess that's a mother's way, but I'll say anytime that Dean was not responsible for all the drugs, alcohol, and pills that were by that time more important to me than anything.

It wasn't long until William wasn't interested in me anymore, either. He was coming home late after work and making up excuses. Here I was again. Where did the love go that I had with William? He wasn't sending flowers. He didn't come straight home to hold me and tell me he loved me. He wouldn't tell me the truth. I had left my husband for this man, embarrassed and humiliated myself, and he didn't love me anymore.

What's wrong with me? That's what I thought, but I sure didn't have any right to throw stones. Even though I cheated on Dean with William, I wanted my man to be faithful to me. It all went back to whoever would hold me and sweet-talk me and make me feel loved for the moment. That's the one I was going to be with. I know that's so wrong, but that's what I did.

The hospital decided to cut out the x-ray tech position on my shift, so I had two weeks to find another job. I drove to Jackson, Mississippi, about 70 miles from Hickory, and got a job there.

One Friday afternoon, I came home and William said he'd been thinking about our relationship and he didn't think it was going anywhere. Although I knew this was true, it broke my heart. I got in my car, a used Mazda 280Z that William had bought, and drove to Birmingham to my mother's house for the weekend.

I didn't tell my mom there was any trouble. I wanted her to think that I was doing well. I showed her my car and my pretty clothes. I told her about the job at the hospital in Jackson.

I didn't even bother to see my son that weekend. He was with Annie and I figured she was now his real mother. I thought I wasn't worthy to see him, and probably he wouldn't want to see me after the way I had dumped him and left. I shoved those guilty thoughts out of my mind.

On Sunday afternoon I headed back to Mississippi. When I drove up to our apartment, my clothes and all my other things were sitting in boxes by the curb. William was moving my stuff out, and there was a pretty blonde girl helping him do it. "Sorry, Janet. It's over. I'm in love with her and have been for quite a while. Didn't mean to hurt you."

I wasn't even divorced from Dean and now William had thrown me out. Devastated, I drove to Jackson that night, went to work the next day, and moved my things into an apartment with some co-workers who offered to let me stay with them for a while. It wasn't great, but it was a place to stay.

One of the guys who lived in the apartment was Rusty. It was no time until Rusty and I were living together. Rusty was a little man, probably 120 pounds or so. He was nice enough, but I didn't have real feelings for him. I was rebounding from William, and Rusty filled the gap. He had two little boys who visited him every other weekend, but in between those visits, we'd be together.

Although William had bought the 280Z, I was helping make the payments. When I left William, I took the car but quit making payments on it, so he came and got it and I was without a car.

I remember one night being high and borrowing a car from someone. I wrecked the car and was afraid the police would come and arrest me for drugs and for having someone else's car. I ran, walked, and hitchhiked back to the apartment and gave Rusty a big sob story about how scared I was and how I didn't know what to do.

The police came the next day, but by then I had sobered up and made up a story about how I borrowed the car and when the wreck happened I was just so confused and didn't know what to do except to come home. When you do drugs, your life just becomes one big, elaborate lie. You tell one lie and then you have to tell another one to explain that lie and you forget your lies and get tangled up in what you've told everybody. When you're sober and not high, you think about what you might have told and you can't really remember, so you don't even know what lies you have to keep telling. The guilt and shame for all these things began to pile on, layer after layer.

At work, I was dipping and dodging. Sometimes I'd call in and say I was sick and couldn't come to work, and sometimes I'd leave early to get some crack and smoke it up before Rusty got home. He was beginning to get tired of all my lies. Our relationship was definitely on the downslide, but the next thing I knew, I realized I was pregnant. I had been gone from William long enough to know that this was Rusty's baby. When I told him I was pregnant, he was extremely upset. Said he didn't appreciate that I'd let that happen. It was my fault. He said I just needed to take care of it, get rid of it. He'd just gotten out of a divorce and had two kids he was paying child support for and he said he wasn't about to have another child.

I don't know exactly what I expected, but this wasn't it. I felt abandoned and betrayed. Even though I was living a life of dishonesty about my crack and putting myself at risk with things like borrowing and wrecking the car, I couldn't look at my life and see how wrong I was. All I could think was that Rusty didn't care for me and didn't want this child. I was scared to have an abortion. I didn't know what I was going to do.

My supervisor at work was an older, divorced woman, and I talked with her about my situation. She gave me the address of a clinic that did abortions cheap. I don't know if she had gone there or just knew about the place, but I was not quite ready for that. I let a couple of months go by without doing anything. Rusty was withdrawing more every day, and when his children came over, I was nothing. It was all about them, and he didn't include me.

I knew it was over. I was alone again. Rusty moved out.

Drinking and drugging had become my total life instead of just a part of it. I was smoking drugs at work several times a day. I'd hear them call me for an x-ray on the overhead page and I'd be in the bathroom smoking my crack. Although I hadn't binged and purged in a long time, I started doing that some too.

What's wrong with me? Why won't any man stay with me? It's always the same. I'm taken in by sweet talk and I think I'm going to be the love of somebody's life, but they never stay. I feel abandoned and let down by everyone. Of course, now I have to acknowledge I've let down almost everybody in my life, too, but I didn't see that then.

So I called the clinic and used my last paycheck for an abortion. I remember sitting in a chair like they have in a dentist's office and getting an IV. There were several other women doing the same thing. I remember getting woozy and feeling a tug down below. When I came to, it was over. I'd done it. I'd murdered my baby.

I didn't want to think about it. I took a cab back to the townhouse and on the way I stopped at the liquor store and bought a bottle of whiskey. Sitting on the floor by myself, I downed the whole bottle that evening. I couldn't face what I had done. I didn't want to take the blame. As far as I was concerned, everybody else was to blame. *Look what they've done to me. Look how I've been abused and abandoned. If someone had only wanted me, I wouldn't be in this situation. I wouldn't have made this choice. They've all pushed me into it, and it's not my fault.*

By myself that night, I got out some pictures of my family. My dad in the army in World War II and Korea, sitting with his buddies. My brother and me when we were children. *Where did my life go? How did I end up here?*

That was 1990, and I had no idea how much further into the darkness of sin's pit I would go. But that night, in that moment, I thought it was the end of the world for me. I got drunk to forget and to numb the pain. I didn't want to feel anything. *Just let me pass out on this floor and I don't care if I ever wake up.*

The next day I called Chuck, the wealthy older man who was interested in me until he knew I had a son by a black man. I hadn't talked to him since we broke up. I told him I was living in Mississippi, had a run of bad luck, and needed some help. As he would do so many times in my life, he immediately came to my rescue.

I didn't tell him I was married and didn't tell him I'd just had an abortion. Didn't tell him I was broke and on crack and alone. Didn't tell him I didn't know where to go or what to do and couldn't pay the rent.

He wired me some money and a bus ticket, so I walked out of that townhouse and left everything there. It wasn't much, just some clothes and a few things I'd managed to get, but I left the family pictures and my wedding pictures. I walked out with nothing, took a cab to the bus station, and returned to Birmingham. By leaving Mississippi I thought I could leave behind all those painful experiences. *I'll go back to Birmingham and start all over again. Everything will be different. Chuck will take care of me for a while.*

Chuck took me to his house and didn't ask many questions. I was trying to think up all the lies I would tell him to explain my situation. Like I said, lies upon lies. Those "secret" sins made me sick but they became easier. I steeled myself against feeling the guilt and shame. I knew I'd get by just as I always had, and it was nobody's business but mine.

I stayed with Chuck a couple of weeks. He offered to help me get a place to stay and find a job. He rented a little upstairs efficiency apartment for me in an older house in Southside a well-known, popular part of the city near some hospitals. I was delighted with my new apartment—it was everything I needed and then some. Chuck paid the rent for a couple of months and paid deposits on all the utilities for me.

All set. Ready to start over. Again.

Chapter 6

SAM, *CHEERS,* AND NO MORE WORK

I started putting in applications in Birmingham. In no time I got a job at a hospital, about ten minutes from my new apartment. I bought a bicycle and rode it to work almost every day. When it was raining, I'd take a cab. I loved that little apartment and thought things were really looking up for me.

I called Mom to tell her I was back in town and that I was seeing Chuck. She was happy about that. She knew Chuck and she had always thought he would be good for me because he didn't do drugs and didn't want me to, either. Mom came to see me and brought some curtains for the apartment.

I asked about David and if I could see him. He was 13 by then and spent a lot of time, especially in the summers, at my mother's house, although he still lived with Annie. David grew up with some pretty big hurts, like any child would who didn't have his parents around. Don wasn't with him much, and I sure wasn't there for him. Don had problems with relationships, too, so David was on the bottom of the list for both his parents. My heart really grieves now when I think about what David went through because of my selfishness.

Mom brought him to see me. He didn't say much and didn't ask many questions about where I'd been or what I'd been doing. I think he was glad to see me, but he probably just didn't know what to say after such a long time. My heart hurt about what I'd done and not done for him. That haunted me for a few days, but I turned it off and refused to think about it.

While I was training at the hospital, I worked days. Almost every day when I got off at 4:00 P.M., I'd walk or ride my bicycle to a little neighborhood bar. It was kind of like the bar on the TV show *Cheers*, where everybody knows your name. We'd talk and laugh and shoot pool. And drink, of course. Sometimes I'd drink a few, and sometimes I'd drink a few too many.

Chuck traveled because of his job, and when he came home on weekends he expected me to be available. So the days and nights during the week were lonely for me. I filled that loneliness during the week as I always had, by drinking and smoking with someone. Someone who would say the right things. Someone to make me feel good. Anyone who would give me some feeling of being cared for. Then, in the morning, I would get up and go to work the best I could.

Every afternoon I'd go to the bar and return home late at night, especially on Fridays and Saturdays. One Friday night, I had just gotten paid and had about $400 in cash. I haven't the faintest idea how I got home that night, but when I woke up the next morning, I didn't have any money. I thought I'd been robbed or maybe lost the money.

I called the bar to see if anyone found any money. No money, of course. My mother loaned me money to live on for the next two weeks, and I also borrowed money from several friends at work. Months later, I put on a pair of jeans and when I slid my hand down in the front pocket, there was my money, all $400.

I loved the bar and the people there. There was a guy named Sam who drew weird dragon pictures while he was sitting and drinking. Sam was a really attractive big man with tattoos and long strawberry-blond hair.

One night, Sam sent me a Salty Dog, my favorite mixed drink, and told Marie, the bartender, to tell me he thought I was pretty. Of course, I drank it and gave him the come-on. When I drank too much I'd get loud and obnoxious. That's what was happening on this particular night. When Sam came over to talk to me, I can't remember what he said, but I was greatly offended and threatened him. I remember telling him that we'd just step outside and settle it.

He thought that was pretty funny. I mean, I was a little woman shaking my fist in the face of this big, burly guy. So he thought I was cute. Next thing, of course, we're living together. We'd meet every afternoon at the bar and then go to my apartment and he'd spend the night. We'd get up the next morning to go to work.

I was in love with Sam. Same story. How many verses is this? I would be with Chuck on the weekends and he would buy me clothes and jewelry and take me to nice places, but I was with Sam during the week. Of course, this meant building a huge network of lies with both of them.

One night I was out with Sam. I had on an expensive outfit that Chuck had given me, a green turtleneck sweater and corduroy pants with a belt. I thought I was hot stuff in that outfit. Well, Sam and I were partying and dancing and drinking, and in walked Chuck. He gave me a piece of his mind and walked out. It was a long time before I saw Chuck again.

I bought a used Toyota from the father of a man at work and paid him $400 for it, so I gave up the bicycle and cabs for a while.

Sam lived with Matt and Maryann, a married couple, and I moved in with them. They had an older house and even though this was in the 1990s, they still lived like hippies did in the 1960s with everybody hanging out and sleeping wherever they could. Their house was a constant drug party. Even their son would come over and get high with us.

Here we go again. Sam felt like the man of my dreams and that I would love him forever. He was jealous of me and didn't mind letting everyone know that I was his girl. His jealousy even somehow made me feel more loved.

Sometimes when I'd get to the bar in the afternoon, he'd be there waiting with a vase full of roses. I was young and pretty, and he was good-looking and strong. Frequently I'd get drunk and rowdy and Marie, the bartender, would tell him, "Take her out of here and don't let her come back for a week." I'd wake up the next morning and ask what happened. Sam would say something like,

"Well, honey, you got in a fight and hit somebody over the head with a pool cue and Marie threw us out. But it's OK. We can go back. I fixed it."

On weekends, we were at the bar when it opened and usually there when it closed. I'd be so drunk I wouldn't remember much of what happened. I think Sam liked taking care of me like that. I think he thought he was taking good care of his woman. Of course, I was usually his drunk woman.

In the bar, I would often notice an exchange taking place, people buying their drugs. The same two or three guys would come in and the deals would go down. It had been a long time since I'd had crack. Since I came back to Birmingham from Mississippi, I had pretty much used only alcohol and marijuana.

One night Sam said, "Why don't we try some crack?" So we got a $25 rock and took it home. Of course, I knew exactly what to do but he didn't, and I didn't let on that I had ever smoked crack before.

I had forgotten how much I liked crack. I really liked it. We began occasionally smoking, but Sam soon decided he didn't like it and didn't want to continue. I wasn't about to give it up now, and I wasn't going to let him tell me what to do. *I pay half the bills here and what I do with the rest of my money is my business.*

So when we'd be at the bar, I'd signal the dope man and meet him in the back by the restrooms. He'd give me my crack and I'd pay him the $25. I'd go in the bathroom and smoke it quickly. Then I'd come out high and be feeling fine for a while. I'd drink and shoot pool and have a great rush from that crack.

Sam and I decided to get our own apartment and move out from Matt and Maryann's, which made it a whole lot easier for me to keep my crack smoking a secret from Sam. Many evenings, we'd go to the bar and drink a while and then come home and I'd cook a big dinner. Sam enjoyed eating and everything he liked was fried. Fried chicken, fried pork chops, mashed potatoes and gravy.

I'd buy one or two crack rocks before we went home and while the food was cooking I'd go to the bathroom and smoke some. Sam would be drinking his beer and watching TV or working on the computer and he wouldn't notice. I'd flip the pork chops and go take a hit. Sometimes I'd say, "Oh, man, I forgot to pick up flour. I'm going out for flour and be back in a minute." Then I'd run down to the bar, make a quick buy, and rush back to the apartment. Of course, I had to stop at the grocery and pick up some flour too.

Sam spent a lot of time drawing his dragons and wizardry pictures. He'd draw as he listened to hard rock music. In the meantime, I'd be in the bathroom smoking crack. Of course, we'd both have a joint and also a beer. That was our life.

I always had a tab going with the dope men. One hundred, maybe even $200 out of my next paycheck. And that was when I was only bringing home about $800 every two weeks. Sam was expecting me to pay half the bills, buy half the groceries, and come up with money for our bar tab every night too. He knew nothing about the drug debts. So I'd say, "Oh, they shorted me on my check, or I had to send David some money this week and I'll make it up to you next week." Lies, lies, lies. Endless lies.

Some changes were going on at work at the hospital. They asked me to switch to the 4:00 P.M. to midnight shift. I did it, but that really messed with my time at the bar. Sometimes even after I got off work at midnight I'd go to the bar, drink a while, smoke some crack, and then go home and crawl in bed with Sam.

Usually I was the only x-ray tech on that shift and the work got heavier and heavier. That combined with my not being able to go to the bar every night really aggravated me. One night I went in and saw all the work that was piled up and just turned around and left. I walked out. Quit without a notice or anything.

I was out of work about a month and Sam took care of us during that time until I got a job at another hospital. Getting a job was never a problem. I knew I could always hire on somewhere.

By the time I started work at this next hospital, my drug habit was full-blown. I owed huge drug debts, which Sam didn't know about, and I also had to do my part on the groceries and the alcohol we drank.

A new problem developed right after I went to this hospital. I was always careful to bathe every morning, but I guess when you've got that much alcohol in your system it just comes through the pores. My supervisor came to me one day and said, "Janet, one of the doctors says he smells alcohol on you." I wasn't drinking at work, but I guess with all I drank at night, the smell stayed on me.

I was furious. "H—, no, he doesn't smell alcohol. I've not been drinking at work." I got defensive and loud and cursed at my supervisor. "What I do on my personal time is none of your business. How dare you say I smell of alcohol? I don't drink in the morning, and I don't drink on the job." And that was the truth. I didn't do that. But I was drinking so much I couldn't wash away the smell.

They asked me to resign unless I agreed to get some help, and I wasn't about to do that. "I don't need help and you can just stay out of my business." Of course, I didn't say it that nicely. I was screaming and cursing and I walked out thinking they needed to get off my back.

My attitude was that I wasn't hurting anybody, so what I did wasn't up for discussion. The truth is that I was hurting everyone I knew by my constant lies and deceit, including Sam. Even though I loved Sam and I knew he loved me, I was so deep into addiction that I couldn't pull out of it. One lie on top of another was the only way I knew to handle everything. I hurt my mother and my son. I hurt the people I worked for who had treated me with nothing but respect and kindness.

Soon after leaving the hospital, I got a job with a mobile medical organization. Little did I know that this would be the last real job I'd have for a very long time. This company serviced nursing homes, retirement centers, and anywhere else needing mobile medical equipment. I drove a van containing a mobile x-ray machine and a ramp so the machine could be wheeled out of the van and inside wherever needed.

I had a beeper and throughout the day I went from one job to another. I guess anybody could imagine what I really did. This was the perfect setup for me. I'd answer a call, get back in the van and make a short run to a drug dealer's for a hit or two while I was waiting on the next call. What could be better?

If the next call came before I finished with my dope business, it would really make me furious. Before I even started work in the morning, I'd drive by one of the dealers in Southside and get a hit to start my day. Then I'd come back during the day whenever I could.

Sometimes when my beeper went off, I'd ignore it until I could get better control and be able to answer the call. I'd make up excuses, "Oh, I was in the restroom and didn't hear the beeper." Every now and then, I'd get my dope "to go" and smoke on the way. Then I'd look in the mirror and see my eyes red and pupils dilated and think, *Whoa, I can't go anywhere looking like this.* So I'd squirt eyedrops in my eyes and chew on breath mints.

I was always hiding and lying. I think that added to the guilt and disgust I was feeling about myself. That is, when I let myself feel anything. Everything was a lie. Everything was deceitful. Everything was wrong and shameful. But, for the most part, I didn't let it bear down on me. I had to have the crack and that was all that mattered.

This was 1992 and I hadn't gotten into the homelessness and prostitution yet, but I was right on the edge. Crack had taken over my life so completely by now that I wouldn't meet Sam at the bar or go home when I was supposed to. I wanted more time to get high, and Sam was an alcoholic but he didn't like crack, so I still had to hide that from him.

Because I didn't always go home, Sam started going around looking for me. That van was pretty hard to miss, so he found out where I was going and what I was doing. He gave me an ultimatum. I could choose him or the dope. Of course, to his face, I'd say, "Oh, honey, I won't do it anymore. I'll stop." But I couldn't stop. I figured I could make up better lies and still keep him.

Then Sam began acting suspicious, not caring as much about where I was or when I came home. Sometimes he didn't come home either. Someone at the bar told me he was seeing someone else.

One time, Sam locked me out of our apartment. I've already said that I had a mean, violent temper and when I was drinking or high, I was even more violent. I banged on the door and screamed for him to open up. He didn't. I balled up my fist and smashed my hand through the window. What a mess! Sam took care of me and wrapped my arm. We couldn't go to the doctor because we were both drunk.

Two or three days later, I realized I was going to have to get medical attention. I ended up having 13 stitches inside and about 20 on the outside. I can't even remember what excuses I gave the doctor, but you can bet I didn't tell the truth.

My injury gave me some time off work. The owners of the mobile medical organization were really nice to me. They liked me and tried to work with me, but they knew something was going on. The job was coming to an end, and I didn't even want to think about that.

My life with Sam was coming to an end too. I had been so happy with him. Yeah, we had our scrapes, but we laughed a lot and had a lot of friends together. Of course, they were drinking and drugging friends, but that's who we were too. We were still getting together with Matt and Maryann at their big house where we had lived for a while. Everyone would be drunk and we'd have big pot parties. We'd play cards and listen to 1970s and 1980s music.

When Sam left, it was like it all blew up in my face. And, as always before, I thought none of it was my fault. Everybody else was doing me wrong. I couldn't see that my lying, deceiving, crack smoking, or unfaithfulness had anything to do with anything. This was the way people lived. Everyone I knew lived this way. Nobody had a right to hurt me the way they did or walk out on me because of what I did.

I wanted everybody to leave me alone and let me do what I wanted to do and what felt good to me. My boyfriends were supposed to put up with it and not expect anything from me. My employers were supposed to look the other way when I wasn't carrying my end of the deal. Nobody had a right to object or question me.

I thought the whole world smoked crack. I saw so many others just like me begging the dope man for a hit when they didn't have enough money to pay for it. I saw couples fighting and drinking and smoking and then they'd make up and go home. Or maybe split for a while and look for somebody else who lived the same way. That was my life, but I thought it was everyone's life.

I expected life with Sam to go on forever, but it ended. Just like I thought the same about William and Dean and Don. Like so many other men that came in and out of my life in those years. Nothing ever lasted. I see now that my so-called happiness was built on things that don't last. Empty, worldly things and feelings that are good only as long as nothing changes, as long as the high lasts. But then there was no foundation for love or life in any of these experiences.

After Sam left, I stayed in our apartment a couple of months, but I couldn't pay the expenses and still buy my crack. I called some people I used to work with and asked to borrow money. I even called a doctor I knew and he met me and wrote me a check for $40. I think I was always a likeable person unless I was drunk and violent. People usually believed me and wanted to help me, even when I was telling them lies or stealing from them. So it was pretty easy for me to take advantage of kind people.

A weird little man named Harry lived in the same apartments. I didn't even know him, but I went and knocked on his door and gave him my usual sob story. "Hey, I'm your neighbor. My man moved out and left me and I wonder if you could loan me a few bucks."

It was apparent that Harry had problems mentally, but I found out that he got some kind of monthly check. He offered to let me stay with him, and he gave me money every month. Actually, we had a friendship for several years.

Before they could fire me from the mobile medical organization, I went and parked the van, left the keys under the mat, and called and told them I quit. Of course, I made it seem like I had the weight of the world on me. "My boyfriend left me, I can't pay the rent, and I can't stand the stress of the work anymore." I never mentioned that I was hooked on drugs and that's why I couldn't keep up with my job.

Although I'd had plenty of experience in borrowing money from friends, I'd never panhandled from strangers before. I still had nice clothes and shoes that Chuck had bought for me, so I'd take a shower, fix my hair, and go out in the neighborhood and ask people for money. "I'm so sorry to ask you this, but I've run out of gas over on the next block and I wonder if you could help me."

I'd go down to the University of Alabama at Birmingham (UAB) campus and catch students as they came out of class. Everybody was always nice. I didn't look like a homeless person or a street woman, even though I actually was. Because I could go to Harry's and clean up and change clothes and wear something different every day, I still looked presentable.

My old Toyota was on its last leg. It needed tires and had a busted windshield. I didn't have money to fix all that, so I called a wrecker service and they gave me $175 for it and towed it away. That provided two days and nights of all the crack and alcohol I could want.

Panhandling became my new occupation. I pretty much worked the UAB area. I'd panhandle from students or anyone walking around the campus. Same stories all the time. "Hey, I ran out of gas," or "My husband left me and I need some money to feed my babies at home." That worked for a while, and every time I'd get a little money I'd go straight to the dope man and get my hit. I even went into classrooms and offices and panhandled professors and secretaries.

But that pretty much played out because I'd catch the same people and not realize it. "Didn't I give you gas money last week? What are you doing here again? Are you on drugs or something?" The campus police got to seeing me around there too much and started telling me to go somewhere else, get out of their territory.

Then an arts center was built downtown and that was a great place to panhandle. Plays, art shows, that sort of thing. This was an upscale place, so the people coming out of there were dressed up and spit-shined. I'd do the old song of "I ran out of gas and I need some help," or maybe, "I had a flat tire and just need a little money to get my car running again." Of course, if they offered to help me change the tire, I had to come up with another lie. But mainly the people had money and they didn't come every day or every week. Each event was a whole new crowd of suckers, as far as I was concerned.

But Wayne, one of my regular dope dealers, knew what I was doing and he said, "Janet, aren't you tired of begging? See, you get $20 or maybe $40. I'll show you how you can get some real money. Are you up for it?" Well, sure, I wanted money. My habit was growing faster than my panhandling opportunities and I needed a lot more money.

Wayne introduced me to a new rung on the ladder down into the dark pit.

Chapter 7

A NEW PROFESSION — AND HOMELESSNESS

Wayne drove me to a motel downtown. It wasn't in the best neighborhood, for sure. It was a one-story, flat structure with the office at the end and a large parking area. Wayne said he would pay for a couple of days' room rent and explain what was happening there. While he was in the office, I noticed a lot of the doors were open, and I could see girls standing in some of the doorways.

Even then I was pretty naïve about what was going on. Wayne took me to my room. It was decently clean with a little table and two chairs in front of a window. Cable TV, a phone, and a little bathroom. Wayne began to explain the plan.

He said, "See, Janet, here's how it works. Guys will drive by and you motion them in or just stand in the door. They'll come up to see how you look and to proposition you or you can proposition them. They'll ask you how much and you name your price."

"My price for what?" I asked.

"For sex, Janet." He began to be exasperated. "Whatever they want. You ask what they want and you set the price. You've got your own room. You don't have to be out in the weather, and I'll bring you food, cigarettes, a bottle, or whatever you need. You don't have to get out and hustle. The men will come here. And soon you'll have your regulars. Well, try it, Janet. The room is paid for two nights."

I thought about it. It might not be so bad. I'd had a lot of boyfriends and thought I'd been in love with some of them. At least now I'd be making some money. Wayne left me with a supply of crack, some cigarettes, and a bottle of wine. Well, how bad could this be? What did I have to lose?

So I sat down at the little table by the window and waited. I didn't have to wait long. White men and black men drove through the parking lot in fine cars and junk heaps. I'd see them go into a room and maybe 30 minutes later come out. I was watching and learning.

About dark, a big white man came to my room. I was sitting there in the window where I could be seen. Come to find out he was a football player at a nearby university. He said, "Are you up to some fun?"

"What do you want?"

"Sex, and I've got $40 for it."

So we closed the door and pulled the curtains. He was extremely rough with me. It was like, "Hey, I paid you for this and I'm going to get it all." I was scared. So many things were going through my head. *Can I really do this? Can I really? He needs to stop hurting me.*

He had been drinking and he started slapping my face.

"Hey, man, this has got to stop." Well, he didn't care what I said. He wasn't finished and he wasn't going to quit. Finally, when I got the chance, I jumped and ran and opened the door. "Get out of here! Get out of here!" I yelled.

"Oh, baby, come on, let's finish. Close that door before someone sees you. I paid you for this. Come on back."

"You didn't pay me for this," I said. "It's over. You've had your $40 worth. Now, get out."

I'm standing there in the doorway, and it's not even dark. No telling how many people saw and heard what was going on, but I didn't care. He hurt me and I wanted him gone. "You need to get out of here or I'm going to holler for help," I said.

I stood there and held the door while he got his clothes on. I wasn't going to let him hurt me anymore. Now if he'd come out with $100, would I? Yeah, I probably would. But he didn't offer any more money and I was through. He left, cursing loudly and threatening to do all kinds of horrible things.

When he was gone, I closed the door and sat on the floor and sobbed. I had never felt filthier. *This is too hard. There's no way I can do this. I'd rather get out of here and panhandle for a few bucks. I'd rather go out there and tell lies all day than to be treated this way.* I couldn't stop crying. How did I get here?

I had just had the meanest treatment you could imagine and I'd made $40 for it. I was supposed to lie there and let this stranger do anything he wanted and cut off all my feelings?

When my crying stopped, I had $40. I could buy a crack rock, a couple packs of cigarettes, and maybe a bottle of wine. I had a bathroom where I could go and wash off the filth and the stench. I would call Wayne and say, "Hey, I've got $40. Bring me my stuff."

After all, I said to myself, *I'm out of the weather. I don't have to beg. Maybe it gets easier. Yeah, that's it. I'm sure it gets easier. This was probably the worst experience I'll ever have. Maybe it is better than walking the streets, begging and telling lies, and looking for a place to sleep at night. Maybe it gets better.*

So I cleaned up and opened the door. And I started all over. I don't remember the rest of that night. I guess I blocked out everything and focused on the money. I made over $200 before morning. Sometime in the middle of the night I called Wayne and said, "Come on over and bring my crack. I'm making a killing! I want something to drink and a couple packs of cigarettes too. I'm handling it and I'm doing good."

I gave in to sin and desire, and I gave in to that voice I heard saying it would be OK. Nothing else mattered now except that I had enough money to buy the crack I needed so badly. Wayne brought me dope, drink, and cigarettes. I had enough for several days. I took a little nap, cleaned up, and got ready for the next day's business. I could do this.

My world was full of sin and perversion. Now it makes me sick to think about it. But then my desire was feeling good and having enough crack to stay high. I'd shut my door between tricks and smoke or drink a little and I'd be ready for whoever was out there. I was paying my rent and Wayne was making a killing off me with all the dope I bought from him.

Some of the other girls started threatening me. It wasn't that I had anything more than they did, but I was the new girl and sometimes their customers just wanted somebody new. Wayne said if anybody gave me trouble I could call him and he would be there in ten minutes.

Sometimes my customers wanted to bring the dope with them. We'd sit and smoke dope. They'd buy it and pay me for us to do it together. That was great! I didn't have to spend my money on dope and we both got what we wanted. I have to honestly say that I met some men who were probably really nice, upstanding people except that they had an addiction to sex, pornography, alcohol, or dope. Or maybe all of those.

They got caught up in sin, just like me, and it became so easy. I didn't have any problem with anything I was doing. I got comfortable with it. Everything was easy and I had a good place to stay. Money rolling in and plenty of dope. I remember thinking, *Why in the world did I spend my time panhandling on the street for a few dollars when this is so easy?*

Before long, the police began to clamp down on our motel. I'm sure the owners knew what was going on, but they had their rooms rented and they didn't care. When the police put the heat on them, the owners told us we would have to go somewhere else, at least for a while. So I moved to another motel. The new one had three floors and you had to go through the lobby and take an elevator to get to the second and third floor. There were security cameras, too, so many men didn't want to come in there.

I was barely making rent money in this new location. Sometimes I'd go downstairs to the bar and find a man who would go up to my room. Other times I would go out and walk down the street and a car would pull over and ask if I was ready for a little fun. I'd hop in and say, "Let's go to my room at the motel."

It didn't take the owners long to catch on to what I was doing. "Your friend comes here too often," or "Why do you have so many friends going up to your room?" They told me to leave. I ended up going back to the Southside area where I'd started out. But now I was on the street.

It was 1993, and this would be the first time I'd actually be homeless—without a regular place to go, to keep my clothes, and to sleep at night—but this is the way I would live for several years.

Southside is a mixture of all classes of people and all kinds of buildings. St. Andrew's Episcopal Church was next door to some green apartments which were my landmark for the area. Many of the drug dealers I frequented operated from these apartments, and it was always a festering hole of drug activity. I knew everyone who lived there, and many times I would hang out in one of the apartments while I smoked my dope. Until my dope or my money ran out, of course, and then they'd kick me out.

One person I would see frequently in that area was a petite young woman with long, brown curly hair. She drove a cute little two-seater red car, and she came to visit some people who lived in the apartments. I later found out that they were missionaries and Kathy Campbell was a member of Grace and Truth Church, which met in a small house near the apartments. Kathy became an important person in my life later on, but I saw her for years before I ever met her.

At lunchtime every day, St. Andrew's church would serve meals to homeless people. Sometimes on weekends other churches came and gave out sack lunches. Most of the time that lunch was all I would eat all day and if I missed it I'd have to wait until the next day to eat. A few times I'd be lucky enough to be in somebody's apartment and they would have food along with the dope and alcohol, but that was rare.

I got good at finding food. Some of the businesses threw away really good food—whole racks of ribs and little side dishes that people hadn't even opened. Dumpster diving for food became my main way to eat other than the church lunches. Also, there was plenty of food thrown out on the road. Frequently I'd find a fast-food sack with a hamburger only half eaten and some cold fries.

I spent my days sitting on the brick wall beside St. Andrew's church. Cars would come along and pull over and the guys would say something to me. I'd jump in the car and say, "Hey, you want some action?"

"Oh, sure, where can we go?" Sometimes they'd have a place to go. Often we'd drive around to the parking lot in back of the apartments and and I'd make my money and go back to the brick wall to wait for the next guy.

People who lived in the apartments were usually ready and willing to rent out a back bedroom for 30 minutes or an hour. I'd get my money, give them a little cut, and use the rest for my crack purchase. Some men would come every day at the same time or the same day every week. There were several men who lived in that neighborhood — married men, of course — who would come by after work for a quick trick before going home.

I had fallen into this drug and prostitution lifestyle without even trying hard. I hadn't tried hard not to get there, either. All I cared about was that I needed the crack and I had to have money to buy it. I would do anything to get money to supply my need.

A lot of people in the Southside area knew me because I had lived there before. They'd say, "Hey, didn't you run that van and take x-rays and work at the hospital? What happened to you?" I didn't want to answer those questions. I'd just say, "Yeah, I got tired of it." I didn't want to face up to how I had lost that life. I didn't want to even remember that life. It hurt too much, so I just closed it out.

Yes, my life had changed drastically. I wasn't working and bringing in a paycheck. I didn't get my scrubs on and go clock in at work and feel important and take pride in my work. I didn't go home at night and cook supper for a man who loved me. I had become a person I didn't know. Didn't want to know. I had stepped across a fine line into a world I didn't know existed and now I was firmly a part of that world. I had no idea how much was ahead of me at this point.

But I knew I could get through this. I could get my hit and forget how I got it or what I had to do for it. I never would have believed how much of my soul I gave away. The progression of sin was a deep pit into which I was free-falling faster and farther every day. But to me, this was tolerable sin. I was fooling myself into believing that. I could forget it, or I could say, *Oh, it really isn't that bad.*

But sin grows. The darkness gets darker. I was so far lost that only God would be able to pull me out. But who was God? What did He care about me? *I'm too dirty for Him. He doesn't love girls that do the things I do.* That's what I thought about God.

Hour by hour, day by day, the web spun tighter around me. I had no thoughts about breaking out. As hard as my life was, I could see nothing beyond the moment. I didn't allow my mind to go there.

Chapter 8

FRIENDSHIP ON THE STREET

I saw a lot of action sitting on the brick wall by St. Andrew's church. You didn't have to be involved in drugs to know what was going on in those green apartments next door. Any time of the day or night, people were cruising through the parking lot. Sometimes they'd park and go in and come out and you'd know they'd gotten their drugs. Dope men would hang out in the parking lot behind the apartments and people would make a deal through the car window.

There was a self-service laundry across the street. If you were doing your laundry, you could call and the dope man would come over and bring your dope. How's that for service? There were two brothers who sold dope and still lived with their mother. They had a room in the back of the house where people would just come up and tap on the window and the brothers would hand their drugs out the window, take the money, and close the window. Drive-through drugs.

Every now and then the police would stage a raid. Sometimes they would arrest a few people, but most of them knew how to get the heck out when they saw the cops coming. Occasionally someone would throw drugs in a trash can if they were being chased. Several times, I got a big bag of dope simply by watching what was happening.

I'm not kidding when I say I would do anything for a hit. One time a dope dealer asked me if I knew a particular woman. I said I did. He told me she owed him a lot of money. She had money, but she was getting all she could on credit and didn't want to pay. So the dope man told me he would give me $20 if I could knock her down with my fist the next time she came. Twenty dollars would buy a good hit of crack, so I watched for her.

When she came walking up to the apartment where the dealer stayed, I casually strolled toward her and, without any warning, I balled up my fist and knocked her to the ground. The dope man came out and demanded his money from her. She was bleeding and crying, but she fished out the money and paid him. He gave me my $20.

So did she leave and not come back? Are you kidding? She went to an ATM, got some more money, and came right back to buy more crack. It's so pathetic, but it's true. When the drugs control a person, you'll do anything. I punched her out for a hit of crack. That's how bad I needed it. And she paid up and went to get more money. That's how bad she needed it.

Another time, I was with a group of five guys and we were all high, laughing and joking about things. One of them told me that if I would climb up on the low roof of the building, take my clothes off and jump off, they would all give me a $10 rock. I did it. I was bruised up a little, but I got my dope. That's how crazy for crack I was.

Watching other people coming and going from the green apartments, driving their good cars, and getting their dope anytime they wanted it, I thought even then that everyone was better than me. Of course, in my other life—before dope got its hold on me—I thought everyone had better families and better opportunities than I did. They looked better, were happier, their husbands loved them more, they had friends, or their parents were better off than mine. And even in this world I'd crossed over to, it was the same. Nobody really loved me. The dope dealers had favorites and I wasn't one. If I had money to buy my stuff, that's fine, but if I didn't, I wasn't one they would front for a few days like they did when I had a job.

I'd see women drive up in their fine cars and spend hundreds of dollars on crack while I had to do anything I could to get $5 or $10 to buy mine. Of course, the dealers would pamper them.

So even in this life on the street, I wasn't wanted or loved. I was so envious.

While I was hanging around the green apartments, there were several people who would occasionally let me sleep in their apartments. Other times, I had to find a place. Sometimes that meant just curling up somewhere against a building or in the basement of an abandoned business.

Parties at the apartments went on day and night. We would spend the night drinking and smoking dope. Someone might pass out or go to sleep for a couple of hours and get right back up and party on.

In all these people I met during that time, I could see hurt and pain. I often wondered what brought them to this place in life. It wasn't always because they intentionally chose this lifestyle. Many times, as I got to know them, I found out that life had been devastating to them and they had just given up. Mostly they started using drugs or drinking a little and it didn't take long for a little to become a lot. From there, it was all downhill.

Friendships on the street are, of course, different than friendships among people who aren't sharing an addiction. One of my best friends about that time was a girl named Lynn, a prostitute like me, except she made better money than I did. She'd come driving along in her blue two-door Ford Gran Torino, like a *Starsky and Hutch* car, and buy $50 worth of crack at a time. I was always lucky to buy $10. Lynn was beautiful. Long black hair, great figure, and always fixed up. To be frank, I was jealous of her. She obviously had it made. Lynn had a mouth on her, sort of like me. She was able to take care of herself and make her deals to get the most crack for her money. She wasn't begging like I was.

One night Lynn asked me if I wanted to go with her to rob an old man. "Sure, sounds fine to me." So we got in her car and drove a long way to a trailer out by itself. We discussed what we would do when we got there. Lynn said since she'd known him and been having sex with him for a long time, I would be somebody new for him and he would be excited about that. So the plan was for me to occupy him while she searched for money and food stamps.

He was drunk when we got there, so it wasn't much of a problem to distract him. I was talking dirty to him and messing with him and got him into one of the bedrooms while Lynn searched his pants and other places in the house. Once he was through with me, Lynn and I changed places and I searched around. I don't remember how much money we took from him, along with some food stamps. When we were through, we hopped in her car and left him passed out and several dollars poorer.

Lynn and I became pretty close friends over the next few years, but this was our first time to pull a scam together and we were kind of checking each other out, I guess. Anyway, when we got back on the highway, she started yelling at me and telling me I obviously had found some money or something that I didn't share with her. She called me a liar.

Next thing I knew, Lynn pulled off on the shoulder of the road, pulled a knife on me, and told me to get out of her car. She was screaming and cursing at me, telling me I had been dishonest with her about what I had gotten off the old man. I got out asking myself *how in the world has this happened*? Whatever we had gotten, Lynn had all of it. She had used me and then taken the whole booty for herself.

I was walking down Highway 78 and a car full of young men came by and asked me if I wanted a ride. They were drinking and laughing. Probably laughing at me, but I didn't get that. It was cold and I didn't have a coat, so I thought, *Well, why not?* I got in the car.

I was joking and laughing with them, and they'd never done anything like this before. Bought a woman, I mean. I made $20 off the guy in the backseat. They thought they were big men now. I knew they were too naive and I had taken advantage of that, but it didn't matter to me. All that mattered was that I had $20 and I was going to get a good supply of crack with that. They took me over to Southside and dumped me out. They left, screaming with laughter.

I went to buy my crack from one of my regular dope dealers. When I walked up to his apartment, I could hear Lynn talking and laughing. When I opened the door, there she was. I knew she'd probably traded the food stamps we'd stolen for crack. She didn't say anything to me at first, but I said plenty to her. Back then, I cursed and used filthy language almost every time I opened my mouth. Filthy language to go with my filthy body and filthy thoughts. All that talk didn't mean anything to Lynn, though. She blew me off.

Sometimes I would see Lynn come to the green apartments in a car being driven by an older man. She would jump out, go make her purchase, get back in the car, and they would drive off. I found out that this was her sugar daddy, Robert. She lived with Robert about four blocks from the dope-infested apartments. I later came to realize that Robert probably really wanted to love Lynn. He gave her money and took her back after she'd leave for days at a time, even though he knew she'd been with someone else.

That was part of the reason I was jealous of Lynn. I always had to really work for my money. I had to have a hit every few hours, and I lived from one $10 rock to the next. I had developed such a craving that I'd do anything. I was out there — bold, rude, crude, surviving, didn't care, would do anything — and everybody knew it. I didn't have a sugar daddy to take care of me. But Lynn and I were friends in a kind of friendship that can only exist between two people who live for the moment. She was sitting pretty with her sugar daddy and she didn't need my friendship like I thought I needed hers.

One time she asked me to go to where she lived with Robert when she said he wanted what she wouldn't do. As I've said, there's nothing I wouldn't do. So I went that time, and occasionally I'd go back to Robert's when Lynn invited me. I think in many ways he kept her sick because he supplied most of the money for her dope and gave her a comfortable place to come home to. He took her in when she was a dancer and a prostitute and made it easy for her to keep up her habit. If she ever overcame her addictions, she might not have needed him any longer.

In a weird way, though, I think they cared for each other. They'd known each other for many years and I guess they were both comfortable with their arrangement. She could buy her dope and then go sit and talk with him while she was high.

Sometimes Lynn would ask me to trick with her. She'd say, "This guy wants two girls, are you ready?" I was always ready, especially because Lynn usually brought in more money than I did so that would help me too. Sometimes after Lynn and I had been together with some guys, I would go to Lynn's house and take a shower and she would give me clean clothes.

As I said, Lynn was beautiful, and she had the opportunity to keep herself up with nice clothes and makeup, all provided by Robert, of course. So she had some advantages that I didn't have. I'd ride with her sometimes when she went to a certain doctor's office to get prescriptions or pills. This doctor would write her any prescription she wanted or give her samples. She laughed about how easy it was. While I waited in the car, she'd go in the back room of the office with him; afterwards he'd give her any prescription she wanted.

Lynn was also on methadone. Robert took her every day to the methadone clinic, and on Fridays she would get enough for the weekend when the clinic wasn't open. Many times she would sell the weekend supply to buy crack. We'd find a couple of men and hang out with them somewhere for the weekend, drinking, getting high. Then Lynn would go home to Robert.

I didn't have that luxury, so that's why I was jealous of her. I would go back on the street and hustle some more to find somewhere to sleep that night by trading myself for a place to be inside. Many nights I'd be on a bench somewhere or curled up under somebody's porch. Sometimes I slept on dirty mattresses in somebody's apartment and there's no telling what had been done on those mattresses and how filthy they were. But it was a place to be out of the weather. Lynn was always fresh and clean while I'd usually be dirty and nasty.

Lynn and I had good times and bad. Sometimes we'd stab each other in the back. She hurt me many times. I wanted a friend and thought she was a friend, but it was only as long as she could use me. Then she was ready to be rid of me.

One time, one of my regular guys got a big check for a settlement on something and he came looking for me. Said he wanted to get a motel room and some booze and drugs and have a great party for two or three days. I asked him if he would like to have two of us and he was all for it. So I called Lynn and told her where to meet us. I wanted to include her when I had a good prospect so she would do the same for me.

We had the room for three days, including nonstop drugs and alcohol. No begging or pleading. It was all available. But the next thing I know, the guy and Lynn are saying I had to leave. Lynn had talked to him and put me down and said, "We don't need Janet; let's get rid of her." As I've said, Lynn was beautiful and had all the opportunity to keep herself up. By this time, I was looking pretty used up. So they talked really rough to me and ordered me out.

I walked back to Southside, crying all the way. I had invited her to come with us and now she talked this guy into turning on me and choosing her. I was so hurt. And so alone.

A couple of days later, the guy came and found me and apologized. He was looking for Lynn because she had ripped him off and stolen his wallet. I have to say that gave me some sort of satisfaction.

Everyday survival on the street was a challenge. Having a job, a home, responsibilities, washing the dishes, raising the kids, going to work, paying bills, cooking supper, making your bed, and going to the grocery store were parts of a dream world that didn't exist for me—even having enough food was always a problem. I was frequently hungry.

I would often smell myself and realize how filthy I was. How could anyone want to be with me when I was so filthy? Sometimes I'd get a bonus and trick with somebody who had an apartment and they would let me take a bath and sleep there for a night or two. I got all my clothes either out of trash piles thrown out on the street or from dumpsters. I almost never had underclothes. Sometimes I'd steal jockey shorts or boxers from some man's apartment.

My cravings didn't sleep at night either, and it was hard to find a dope dealer to buy from in the early morning. Usually they sold out during the night and went to bed in the early morning hours, so someone like me who needed a hit every few hours was out of luck in the mornings. I'd go from one dealer to another. "I'll get back to you, Janet. I'm sold out. Come back later." Of course, my little $10 or $20 purchase wasn't enough to make them care if I came back. I was always desperate for what I needed. Like a lion looking for prey or a deer looking for water. No matter what time it was, I had to have it.

Pretty much all the dope dealers were users too. I would frequently exchange favors for drugs from them. One particular dealer, Carlos, was always willing to barter with me. One day we were in the back room of his place and, as he was leaving the room, he dropped a large bag of crack, but he didn't know it. I was too scared not to take it back to him, but I was fearful even then. I knew if I didn't return it, he would beat me up. If I did, he might accuse me of taking a rock out of it and beat me anyway.

I didn't take even a tiny rock out of that bag, but I trusted that he would give me some as a reward for returning the bag. Nothing. He gave me nothing. I believe even then I had a conscience. Although I was daily living in deep sin, I often wanted to be fair and honest and treat other people well.

As I had all my life, I wanted love. I wasn't crazy enough to believe that all the men I laid down with loved me. And even Lynn or any of the other girls out there were only my friends as long as the good times rolled. The dope dealers weren't my friends, either. I thought that after a while of buying from the same dealer I could say, "Hey, I'm short today but I'll bring it to you tomorrow if you'll front me a hit." But, no, they didn't do that. "Janet, get out of here and come back when you've got the cash." Even though there were people around all the time, life was extremely lonely.

I don't think I really ever hated anyone during my years on the street, not even when they used me and cast me aside like Lynn did several times. I wanted to hate them and for the moment I did, but I didn't have anything else to hold on to except the people I knew and the life that I knew with them.

I spent a lot of time jumping in and out of cars, being driven somewhere in back of an apartment building to turn a trick. It didn't matter who it was. It didn't matter if I didn't know them. If he had the money, I'd go. Then they'd bring me back to my regular place on the brick wall by St. Andrew's church and I'd wait for the next customer.

For a brief time, I did have a place to stay, with Sims. Sims, a cab driver in the Southside area, was a skinny, unattractive little guy, but he would let me hang out at his place, so he was someone I could use for a while. He was sort of sweet on me, but he never did ask me to stop prostituting. He wanted me to be available for him when he came in from work, but he didn't much care what I did during the day. Still, I couldn't sit around and wait for him to come home and bring some dope because I needed it often, not just once a day.

While I was staying with Sims I was served with an arrest warrant on an old traffic ticket. That time I got probation, but I never reported to my probation officer, so it wasn't long until the cops saw me walking down the street and arrested me on a failure to appear in court. During my years on the street, I was in jail for 17 various charges, all misdemeanors for a bad check, traffic charges, minor thefts, assault, soliciting, and several traffic offenses like speeding, not having a valid license tag, and failures to appear in court.

Life was wearing me out. I was very tired. It would be years before I would find rest. I was learning that friendships on the street weren't real, but I was still looking for a place to fit in. I tried really hard to fit in. The dope dealers were my masters. "Janet, run down and get me some cigars so I can make a blunt. Janet, go buy me a pack of cigarettes. Janet, that girl owes me $20; go slap her around and get my money for me."

Why would I let anyone treat me that way? Because when I did, I got a free hit. That's what life was all about.

Thoughts often raced through my mind. *I wonder about my mom. Is my son OK? I wonder if I ever see anybody that knows me and tells my mom what I'm doing. Do people I worked with drive home from work this way and see me hanging out with the druggies? Would they even recognize me?*

I already believed that my family or the people I used to know and work with didn't care anything for me. I knew I was just trash to them at this point. And most of the time I felt like trash to the people on the street too. There were very few who treated me with any human respect or actually had a heart and cared.

I was really still like that 13-year-old girl craving affection and attention. These men never filled the need for affection, love, or belonging for me. They only supplied the way to get what I wanted, drugs or a drink. I began to hate them all, including myself. I hated every minute of it.

Chapter 9

HOMELESS AND
PREGNANT – AGAIN

Two important changes came about during this time. Sims and I moved to a hotel downtown, and I realized about the same time that I was pregnant. This was 1994, and my son, David, was 19 years old. It had been a long time since I had seen him or my mother. Now and then I would call her and when I'd hear her voice, I'd hang up. I didn't know what to say. I didn't know what David was doing or how he was getting along.

I'd only been pregnant two times before, when I had David and when I had the abortion in Mississippi. I'd never used birth control, so it's amazing that I hadn't been pregnant countless times. I had no way of knowing who the father of this baby was. For a fleeting moment, I wondered if I could have this baby and be a good mother. I carried a certain amount of guilt about not being a mother to David and, certainly, about aborting my unborn child. Now that I was older, maybe I could do it better. I knew I couldn't have another abortion. On one hand, after the abortion, I felt a huge sense of relief, but, on the other hand, I still knew that abortion was murder and I couldn't kill again.

Satan can sure fill us with lies, though. I kept thinking, *Remember how good it felt after the abortion to be free of that responsibility and to be able to start over? It was the right thing to do. You couldn't take care of that baby then and you can't take care of this one.*

But I also believe God was speaking to my heart and telling me that I couldn't do that again. Even now, years later, tears come to my eyes when I think of what I did to my unborn baby. I wonder what it would have been like if I'd had that baby. At least, that child would have had a chance at life.

So here I was, faced with another pregnancy.

It didn't take long until my breasts were growing, along with my appetite, but the cravings for alcohol and drugs never stopped and I never slowed down on anything I was doing. At first, the men didn't know I was pregnant. When it became obvious, most of them didn't care as long as I did what they wanted. I wasn't willing to think about what all this might do to my baby. The only person I thought about was me. I blocked everything else out completely.

Even though Sims and I had moved to a hotel downtown, I still played all ends of town where I knew there was any activity. I'd do a trick and then have that guy drop me somewhere I could get a hit, do another trick, and move on.

Our new hotel home was like nothing I'd ever encountered. A few rooms had a bathroom, but most of the rooms, like ours, had only a bed and a sink. There was a community bathroom with toilets and showers at the end of the hall. Rooms were rented by the day or even by the hour, so pimps and prostitutes used those rooms by the hour or perhaps overnight. The smell of crack would drop you down.

While Sims was out at night driving his cab, I'd do my usual business. It was easy with all the men coming and going. Since I didn't have a pimp, I caught a lot of flak from the other women. I got to keep all the money I made and they had to give their pimps most of what they made.

There was no prejudice here. Anything went. Black pimps with white girls, white pimps with black girls, homosexuals. It didn't matter. There was a lesbian who worked in maintenance at the hotel and she had lots of girls on crack who would hook up with her. She had a son who played guitar on the street and he would get some money and come back with some dope. I'd hang out with him and help him smoke his dope. I could always find a customer and a way to get high. Dope was available everywhere.

Several of the pimps had approached me about leaving Sims and coming with them. "You don't need that guy. Come with me and you'll make the big money. I'll supply you with all the dope you want." Of course, what they wanted was for me to get out there and hustle and then they would get a big part of the money for their own dope. They're all dopers and they make their girls do the work. The pimps give the girls only small portions of what they take in.

One day I looked outside to see one of the pimps beating a girl. He was screaming at her that she didn't charge enough. "I told you to get $50 and where's the other $10? Are you holding out on me? I'll teach you, you . . ." I didn't belong to any of the pimps, but this scared me, anyway. Maybe it was time for me to leave, but I couldn't think about leaving when I was making money and getting all the dope I wanted.

It wasn't long, of course, until my pregnancy started showing. People would ask me if I was pregnant and I'd say, "Oh no, just gained a little weight, you know. Don't walk around much anymore. Just a little weight gain."

Being a little older with this pregnancy may have had an advantage for me because even though I still did almost everything I had been doing — drinking, drugging, and tricking — there were some things I wouldn't do. I met people who tried all kinds of things to get high or to enhance their pleasure or fantasies. There was something going on then called Locker Room where you snorted some kind of liquid through a napkin and it made you black out for a few minutes. I wouldn't do these kinds of things. I guess that's a crazy standard that I would drink and drug but wouldn't do other things because it might hurt my baby, but that's the way I thought.

One night Sims came home and wanted me, as usual, but I didn't want to. He was smaller than me but really forceful, and he insisted. My years on the street had taught me how to handle myself. Being bigger than him didn't hurt either, so we tied up like two guys in a barroom brawl and fought it out on the floor. I bloodied his nose and beat him up pretty well. He ran out to the car screaming at me to get out of the room. "Be outta here when I get back, b—." Of course, everybody around heard us because the walls were paper thin, and they were all laughing.

So now I was homeless again. And pregnant.

Even before Sims threw me out, I had been thinking about contacting my mother. I hadn't talked to her in a really long time. I didn't know what to say or how to say it. I wondered how she was doing and what was going on with David. I thought about them and my brother, but I didn't have the guts to face them.

I didn't want to remember. I didn't want to think, *Hey, maybe they do still love me. Maybe she would take me back. Maybe I could clean up my life. Maybe it's not too late.* When I had those thoughts, Satan was right in there too. *No, you can't. They'd never forgive you. Just look at yourself! You're hopeless.*

And then a man would come along and make me an offer I couldn't refuse. I was so deep in sin and so lost that I couldn't say no because I knew it would supply the crack I couldn't seem to live without.

But when I landed back on the street, I decided to call my mom from a pay phone. Her reaction was pretty much what I expected. "My God, not again! You can't come home. I can't help you raise another baby and go through what I did with David. You'll have to figure something out." And she hung up on me.

That same day, I got picked up on a misdemeanor arrest warrant and served a few days in jail. When I got out, I called Mom again. By then, I guess she'd had time to cool off. She said she couldn't come to get me but if I got a ride, I could come home. I hitchhiked to Trussville, a town close to Birmingham, where she lived in a trailer park.

When she came to the door and saw me, she looked stunned. I can only imagine the pain of seeing her daughter looking like a dirty, disheveled, homeless person. That's exactly who I was. She immediately wanted me to take a bath and she gave me some of her clothes. I saw her go in and disinfect the tub and commode when I was finished. I guess she didn't know what kind of diseases or varmints I might have brought home. She also washed my clothes in disinfectant.

Mom immediately started telling me that I couldn't stay there. She reminded me that she had very little income and couldn't afford to help me. I told her I just wanted a place to stay for a little while. I asked about my brother, but she said he didn't want anything to do with me. I guess I understand how he felt. He had been there to help Mom and they didn't even know how to contact me if they needed me. He was resentful.

When I got to Mom's, I was so hungry. I mean, deep hunger. I hadn't eaten in several days, but, really, I hadn't eaten well in a long time. Sims was a little, skinny guy and he didn't eat much, at least not when we were together. Besides that, when you're living from one hit to the next, food isn't the most important thing. So when I got to Mom's, I ate like a hungry puppy. I couldn't get full.

For a few days I did nothing but eat and sleep, but Mom made it plain she didn't want me there permanently. When I'd had time to rest up, I looked for social services in the phone book. I wanted to do something about this baby growing in me. I didn't think I could go through another abortion, but I just didn't know what to do.

Chapter 10

A SAFE PLACE, GOD, AND THE SAME OLD ME

After several fruitless phone contacts with social service agencies, I got an appointment with a counselor at Catholic Family Services. I didn't know what would happen. I figured they might pray over me and wish me luck.

Here I was, 34 years old, pregnant, homeless, a prostitute, in and out of jail, with several nicks and scars from fights I'd been in. I still had most of my teeth but many were in bad shape. Of course, dental hygiene was nonexistent and my teeth were rotten from the drug use and neglect. Mom gave me a shirt and pants of hers to wear to the interview. I didn't have panties or a bra, but I was clean.

Sarah, a pretty, black-haired young woman, welcomed me with a smile and seemed genuinely glad to see me. She asked me why I had come to Catholic Family Services. I explained that I was pregnant and my mother wouldn't let me come back home. I told her my boyfriend left when he found out I was pregnant. Yeah, I told Sarah a few lies that day. I told her I used drugs occasionally and drank alcohol some. I sure didn't tell her that I was completely homeless, a drug-addicted prostitute, and that my boyfriend was as much of a mess as I was.

After we talked for a while, Sarah asked me if I would be willing to go to a home, a safe place, where I could stay for the remainder of my pregnancy and for a while after giving birth. Then I would have time to make a decision about whether I wanted to try to keep this child or make a placement for the child. She said if I decided to keep the child, they would help me find a place to live and get back on my feet. If I decided on placement, they could handle that by finding a good family for my baby.

I told her I definitely would like to go to this safe place and that I wanted to make a placement for the child. She stressed that I didn't have to decide immediately. She said I would be in a good environment where I could receive prenatal care and nutritious food for the rest of the pregnancy. That sounded good to me.

Suddenly I felt very tired. Used up. I wasn't proud of myself. I was pregnant for the third time and still totally unfit to be a mother. I was looking for a way out. Was I afraid to be a mother? Was I listening to Satan and letting him keep me down?

All I could think about was that I knew I couldn't care for a baby, couldn't listen to the crying, and couldn't be responsible for another life. Satan had me fooled into thinking that I could just give this baby up for placement and start over. I mean, it wasn't like I had just gotten a little off track and was going back into a wonderful situation. I pretty much knew I would have this baby, give it up for adoption, and then return to my old life.

The next day Sarah picked me up and took me to Hannah Home, a women's shelter near Odenville, Alabama. On the way, we stopped at a Walmart and she gave me a $75 gift card from Catholic Family Services to buy anything I wanted. I bought two sweatsuit outfits, a bra and panties, some tennis shoes, a little makeup, and some shampoo. I couldn't remember the last time I'd had that much money to spend. It had been years since I'd had my own makeup or shampoo. I was getting real happy with this new situation. I can't say enough about Catholic Family Services and all they did to provide for me and show love and compassion for me and my unborn baby.

After shopping, we drove out in the country and went down a long, dirt road to a beautiful, large brick home. I met Lucy, the supervisor, and Leslie, a counselor. They made me feel right at home. Lucy had a sweet voice and was so nice to me that I thought she couldn't possibly be for real. During my stay there, I found out she was certainly for real. She and her husband, Jerry, were fine Christians who had a profound influence on the women who came through that home.

Leslie was more of an in-your-face personality. She was a country talker, and would tell you the way it was with no reservations. She and her husband, Garrett, were also wonderful people who made me feel instantly comfortable there.

I was assigned a twin bed in a room with three other young women. We started every day with a hearty breakfast and a Bible study. Then we each had chores to do. Bed call was at 8:00 and lights out at 9:00. There was a living room with a TV, but we were only allowed to watch Christian channels. We cooked our own meals and always had plenty of food.

A few days after I arrived at Hannah Home, I was taken to a local medical center for prenatal care. I found out I was three and a half months pregnant and was given a supply of prenatal vitamins. I told them I had used crack a few times, that I never drank alcohol, and that I had smoked some marijuana here and there. Half-truths and outright lies.

All the girls got along pretty well. We'd have an argument or conflict every now and then, but it was basically smooth sailing. I started seeing this time as a break. It had been pretty rough out on the streets for the past few years, and this was an easy life. Bible studies, chores, nourishing food, watch a little TV. *I can do this.* I settled very comfortably into this new life.

The Hannah Home is supported by sales from the Alabama Thrift Stores, resale shops stocked by donations of clothes, shoes, furniture, and other items. Occasionally we were given vouchers for the local store. I used mine mostly to buy more clothes. I was beginning to feel like I was leading an almost normal life. I had pleasant surroundings, new clothes, and plenty of food. I did my chores without complaining.

All this time, I was hiding my addiction. I certainly didn't want anybody there to know my past, so I put on a good front. When the girls found out I was a college graduate with an x-ray license, that got me some attention. I think Lucy and Leslie started thinking maybe I had a chance at returning to a good life. So I played it up. I made it seem like I simply had some bad breaks in life instead of me making bad choices. I made it sound like *poor, pitiful Janet; she's had some really bad luck. Love gone wrong and now she's here waiting for her baby to be born, but surely none of it was her fault.*

All the people who worked at Hannah Home were radiant Christians. We often had visitors who came and taught a Bible study or preached, and we all went to a local church on Sunday. The people at church knew we lived at Hannah Home, and they treated us with great love and kindness.

I know there was a part of me even then that wanted the peace and joy I saw in these believers. Considering what my life had been up to then, though, I didn't think it was mine to grasp. I thought these people were so perfect and there was no way I could be perfect. I also wondered how they could believe in something or Someone they couldn't see or touch. They believed words written in a book, but how did they know that was true? I had many questions in those days.

I listened when they taught about Jesus dying for our sins, but I didn't understand it and didn't know if I could accept that. I'm sure I thought He wouldn't accept me. I certainly wanted to be like these people, so loving and so faithful, but I wasn't there yet.

This safe life at Hannah Home was good for a while, but I wasn't ready for any permanent changes in my life. I wanted to do whatever was necessary to get by and stay here until this baby was born and then return to my life. Did I ever think about changing? Maybe it passed through my mind from time to time, but I didn't really think it was possible.

Did I ever think about God or wonder if He cared for me? I knew He didn't. How could He care for someone as dirty and filthy as me? I didn't know much about God, but I thought I knew enough to know He wouldn't have any use for anyone like me. Although I sat in Bible study every morning and had all the good influence around me, still I had no real understanding about God.

What I know now is that even though I didn't make any decisions then about changing my life, many seeds were planted in my heart which would grow into a harvest in a few years. I didn't know then about planting seeds, but I look back on that time and those people and how they loved me. Tears stream down my face as I think about how they influenced my life with their faithfulness. They shared their faith with me, whether or not I was ready to receive it. Years later, I remembered that love and faith and knew God used that time as a starting point for drawing me to Himself even when I wasn't ready.

In addition to Lucy and Leslie and their husbands, a woman named Carole worked at Hannah Home on weekends. When she came that first weekend I was there, we recognized each other. We used to both buy our dope at a particular motel that had been turned into apartments. Carole was a tall, big-boned woman with a soft, sweet voice. She wore her brown hair cut short and always wore lipstick. Carole and I talked about the old life.

She told me that several years earlier she had "found the Lord," as she described it. She had become a Christian and Jesus had completely changed her. She told me how she now had a full and wonderful life in serving Jesus. This kind of talk was completely beyond my understanding, but I listened because I could see that something was very different about Carole. She had a whole new being, softer and sweeter.

But here I was, the same old Janet. Maybe even worse because I was pregnant again and waiting to give away my baby. Carole didn't put me down at all. She continued to love me and tell me about Jesus the whole time I stayed at Hannah Home.

At that time, I had no understanding about sin. I thought of sin in degrees. Certainly, I wasn't in the kind of sin I had been for much of my life, so this must be OK. I had no awareness that any sin grieves the heart of God. I thought of pleasing God in terms of being good or being bad. I knew nothing about His grace and love. That was because I didn't have the Holy Spirit living inside of me like I do now. Then I was just proud of myself for not living the kind of life I'd lived for so long.

On a Wednesday night, I went into labor. Leslie took me to the hospital. On the way there, she was talking to me about how I was doing the right thing by making a placement for my baby through Catholic Family Services. In the last few months, so many people had told me that I would make some family really happy, and the baby would have a better chance at life in a family.

Satan was also speaking to me in those days at Hannah Home. *You've given away one child and had an abortion. What makes you think you could even raise a child? You're no fit mother. Don't even think about what you're doing. Just have that baby and walk away. You can do it!*

That's what I wanted to do. Just get it behind me and go on. And that's what I did. When I was on the delivery table, everyone was giving me directions and I was breathing and pushing. I remember hearing a nurse say, "Oh, you've got a little boy! He's got a head full of black hair!" Steven was born on March 7, 1994.

My baby boy was like David. Brown skin and jet black hair. A stout little guy, 7 pounds and 12 ounces. I held him and touched his fingers and toes and checked him out. But I knew he wasn't mine. *This is what I have to do,* I thought. *I've already made the arrangements. There's no way I can be a mother.* That's what I was thinking as I touched him and held him.

I was still so filled with sin, refusing to open my heart to God, just thinking my own thoughts. I was sure I knew what was best, and, most of all, I knew what I wanted. Me, me, me. I wanted to go back to my mother's house where I could smoke cigarettes and drink beer in the afternoon while I lay out in the sun. I could work a couple of days a week for a little extra money and do whatever I wanted the rest of the time. I could start life over. My way.

All those things I'd been hearing in the Bible studies at Hannah Home about how God provides for us in our weakness, and how I can do all things through Christ who strengthens me — I didn't believe any of that. There wasn't any way I could care for this child. It was easier to walk away and think I was doing a good thing for him and for some family. I held him and fed him and hugged him. But I had no thoughts of taking him home with me.

On the third day, the foster family came to get him. I met them. Nice people. They brought a little warm outfit for him, and they made a videotape of him in the hospital for the adoptive parents. I hugged him and told him good-bye. But I didn't cry. Who me, cry? Why would I do that?

But the minute they left the room, I was empty to the bottom of my toes. I walked to the window and watched them get in the car and drive away. I had failed again.

Explain this to me, Lord. Why did I have another baby just to give him away? It hurt so bad I thought my heart was going to break. *But hold on, Janet. Get a grip. It's over. I can't let it get to me. I've got a new life to start. The door is closed on this one. It wouldn't have worked anyway. It's too late. I couldn't do it. Forget it, Janet. Get on with your life.*

I had gotten back in touch with my former lover, Chuck, who was wealthy and always wanted to believe the best of me. I told him I was pregnant, and I sure made it sound like, oh, poor me, how could this have happened? I laid it on thick about how I had changed and I knew it would be best for this baby to be placed with a good family. I told Chuck I was going to start a new life. Of course, he bought it hook, line, and sinker, as he had many times before.

The people at Hannah Home had taken me to various medical facilities to put in job applications and I got a job at one working two days a week. Medicaid paid for some dental work, an eye exam and glasses, in addition to all the prenatal care. When I contacted Chuck, I told him I had a job and he came to visit me and brought me a car—a cute little red Grand Am. So I was looking good, driving a flashy car, and visiting Chuck on weekend passes.

Chuck was always there to pick up the pieces and I was always the manipulating, deceiving liar. I was just living for the moment and that meant enjoying my surroundings and taking everything he was willing to give me. I was living a double life.

The people at Hannah Home talked a lot about God having a plan for everyone. *Well, God, what's Your plan for me? Is it to hurt like this? Is it to always fail at everything?*

I never stopped to pray that God would help me know His will. I never said, *God, show me what to do in this situation. Can I be a mother, Lord? If it is Your will, God, I'll keep this little boy and raise him.* No, I never said any of that. Satan's voice was much stronger inside me than the voice of God. I made the choice based on what I wanted and then blamed God for not providing for me.

So I buried another painful time in my life. One more boulder on the big rockpile of sin and failure that, by now, was overwhelming. Another time I disappointed everyone in my life, including myself. The pit I was in was getting deeper and darker all the time. Satan would pull me toward the world, tempting me with a boyfriend and a car and thoughts of things I could have in that life. But I never fought against Satan. I never said, *God, help me! With You, I can do it! With You in my life, I know I can change!*

There are three voices in every life. One is the voice of the Holy Spirit that convicts us of our sin. That's the voice that pricks your heart in the middle of your pain and makes you know He loves you even in your darkest moments. This voice leads you on to forgiveness and makes you know you're not alone.

And then there's your voice that says, *Oh, I want this or that and I'm going to have it. This is my plan.*

Then there's the voice of Satan, the tempter's voice. He says, *Listen to me. It's not that bad. What you did was really OK. Just don't think about it. Get on with your life. It's what you want that matters.*

I was listening to Satan's voice. Anyway, I sucked it up and got over any guilt I felt about placing my baby for adoption. In a few days I was ready to leave Hannah Home. Some people wanted to pray with me and talk to me about what a hard time I was going through. Others never mentioned a word about my baby. Just acted like it never happened. That's what I did, too, most of the time. Acted like it never happened.

It was a dream, a bad dream, and it was over.

Chapter 11

BACK ON THE STREET

A few weeks after the birth of the baby, I left Hannah Home and went to live with my mother again. I still had my part-time job, was working on getting a good tan, and staying with Chuck on weekends. He was taking me to expensive places and buying me nice gifts.

Mom didn't really know what to think about all this, but I think she was glad I had a part-time job and someone to hang out with. Mom always wanted for me to have the kind of happiness she never had and to live with a good man. With Chuck, she knew I'd be taken care of.

When I was lying in the backyard trying to get a better suntan and drinking my beer, she was glad it wasn't something worse than beer. When I got my paycheck, I'd give her some money to help with the groceries. Chuck paid for almost everything I needed or wanted.

I thought I was pretty special. I had a boyfriend, a snazzy car, and a little job with a paycheck. Nice clothes and all the cigarettes I wanted too.

But it was only a matter of time.

Chuck never came around or called during the week. I only saw him on weekends, and that began to get old. I wanted somebody to love me seven days a week. Chuck never said he loved me. That wasn't in his vocabulary. He bought me wonderful gifts and took me to nice places, but our relationship was all on his terms.

I began to get lonely. I loved being around people and having lots going on, so working a couple of days a week and staying at

Mom's house was not the life I had in mind. I wanted to belong to somebody and have somebody belong to me. Several times before I'd thought I had that, but it never worked out. I wanted to try again.

So I decided to go back to that bar where Sam and I hung out so much. I'd heard that Sam had another girl now, a serious relationship.

In the meantime, I had gotten in contact with Harry, the guy I had lived with earlier, and given him a story about how I was doing better and making something of myself. He had sent me $1,000. I took that money and went to the bar by myself. I was going to show everybody how well I was doing with all the beautiful gold jewelry Chuck had given me and my fine little red car.

Things hadn't changed a lot. I knew almost everyone there, and they knew me. *Hey, here's Janet, and doesn't she look fine.* I set up the bar with a couple of rounds. I was full of myself. Spending my money and flashing my jewelry.

I really wanted Sam to see me now. He knew what I'd become, a homeless crack addict and prostitute, so now it was time to let him see the new Janet. Sam was there with his girlfriend, and I showed off big time. Before the night was over, I'd spent at least half of that $1,000. I was buying drinks for everybody and tipping the bartender with 20s. Really being the big shot. Prideful and arrogant. The "new" Janet was a fake. I looked good because Chuck had showered me with gifts and because I had a little money, but nothing had really changed.

I don't remember everything that happened that night, but I do know I ended up in a crack house. The new Janet was gone. The old Janet was at the crack house with all the other losers.

Reaction to crack is just the opposite of being drunk. A few hits wakes you up and you're zooming, speeding, wide awake, pupils dilated, eyes like teacups. *Oh, my God,* I said to myself. *What in the world have I done? How did I end up here? What's going on?* Six months at Hannah Home and almost three months since I left and I hadn't had a real hit in all that time. I'd been drinking since I returned home, but I hadn't done any drugs other than marijuana while I lay outside working on my tan in my mother's backyard.

Now here I was, drugging it up and loving every minute of it. I had the feeling I'd made one of the biggest mistakes of my life. Although I'd been relatively drug-free for nine months, I hadn't made a decision to *leave* drugs. Since coming home, I hadn't renewed contacts with people from my past, so I hadn't faced any particular temptations. Until I went to the bar that night, I had only avoided other drugs because I hadn't put myself in that environment. It didn't take but one night for me to plunge headlong into the same pit I'd left months earlier.

I was sane enough to think, *Well, maybe I'll just have a few hits and go home and that will be it. I'll enjoy the night, and then I'll be back at Mom's and take up where I left off with work and Chuck and a new life.*

It never happened. I didn't go back home. I never went back to my part-time job, and I didn't contact Chuck. I stayed right where I was and smoked and drank to my heart's content. That little voice that so often taunted me said, *Oh, you like this, don't you? It's too late. You can't change. Why stop now? Get some more. It's your night. It's your life. Who are you hurting? Nobody out there really cares about you, anyway. Do what you want, Janet. Live it up!*

So I did. For a couple of days. While the money lasted, I had all the crack I wanted. A few days later, I woke up to find that, in addition to being broke, I'd traded all my gold jewelry for crack. The beautiful necklace that Chuck had given me probably got me a dime rock. The gold bracelet and the ring . . . who knows? Maybe two hits.

And the car. In my drugged stupor, I'd traded the car for a few hits. Some of the drug dealers were out in my cute car, probably driving around and showing it off while I was getting kicked out of the house because I was out of money or things to trade.

The two guys who ran the house were threatening me and saying I had to get out or come up with some more money if I wanted to stay. I ended up in the back bedroom with one of them. He told me if I gave him what he wanted, he would give me another hit. After all, I'd done this plenty of times before. It had been nine months since I'd gotten myself into this predicament, but I couldn't say it was anything new for me. So there I was, doing what I needed to do for the next hit.

And so the life began again as if I'd never left. Was it degrading? Oh yes. But, so what? I could block it out. I could get over it. It was a nasty situation, but the dope meant more to me than cleanliness or dignity. I was back in the pit of the filthiest, most disgusting life imaginable. But I had my dope. At least for the moment, I did.

The next day, with no money and nothing left to trade, they made me leave the crack house. I was craving, begging, hungry, and desperate. And I was on the street again. I'd find a quick trick, make $10 or $20, buy another hit, and go back out to do it all over again.

I was back in my old stomping grounds, so it wasn't hard to find people I knew. "Oh, Janet, what are you doing? You look great. What about the baby?" I'd say, "Oh, he's with my mother." I didn't want to say I'd placed a child for adoption. Now, what kind of logic is that? I was ready to do crazy stuff for my dope, but I didn't want to admit to placing my baby for adoption.

In no time, Chuck realized what was happening. Because he knew my old hangouts, he came looking for me. Actually, I guess he was really looking for that cute red car I had given up for a few hits of crack. He found it outside another crack house. He saw three young guys drive up in the car and go in, and he called a wrecker to come and get the car. He told me later the guys came out and threatened him, even pulled a gun on him. That wasn't the kind of life he lived, so I know that was upsetting and scary for him.

When I didn't come home or go to my job, my mother and brother and people at work were concerned for me. I was on the street one day during that first week and my brother came driving up in his truck. I was out looking for a date to get some more money to buy crack, but I sure didn't want him to know that. He knew anyway.

"Janet, come on. Get in the truck and come on back home."

I cursed and screamed at him. "Get away from me. Leave me alone. You don't know anything." Then I asked him for money, and I think he gave me $10.

"What am I going to tell Mother?"

"Well, tell her you didn't find me." I knew he'd go back and say, *Janet's on the street again. There's nothing you can do for her.* I was sick at heart for what I was doing. I couldn't stay on a straight path. The drugs were more important than family or friends or security or stability. Drugs were my life.

What was I going to do? Go home and say, *Well, I messed up again. I failed again. I lost my car and probably my job by now. Mom, will you give me another chance? One more chance?* I just couldn't do it. Once again, I chose the low road.

The cravings were every bit as strong as ever. When I'd get a hit, I could forget it all. When I got drunk, I could block it all out. I wanted the drugs and drink to take me away and that's what happened. Why try? I loved this life, and it loved me. So there I was again, hopping in and out of cars, making $5 or $10 or whatever I could just to get the next hit.

I knew how to survive. I knew what I had to do and how to do it. That little voice inside me said it again. *Don't worry, Janet. This is your life. Don't even try anything else. This is where you belong because you're not worth anything more.*

Satan had a boatload full of lies for me, and I bought them every one.

Chapter 12

THE POWER OF ADDICTION

During that first week back on the street, I got into the car with a big dude who said he wanted to go somewhere private.

"OK, I don't have an apartment, but we can go inside this deserted building if you want to."

We never made it inside the building. He drove to the lot in back of the building and stopped the car. Quick as a flash, he opened the glove compartment and out came a little black gun.

"Get over here and do what I want!" he said. He shoved the gun behind my ear and cocked the trigger. I was scared and crying and begging him not to shoot me. There was no one around to hear me cry or scream, but I knew he would kill me in a minute if I made any noise.

When he finished with me, he opened the car door and shoved me out. "Run!" he said. "I may shoot you in the back. I'm going to think about it while you're running."

Well, I barreled out of that car and raced away, crying and shaking. I knew I was going to get shot. No one would see. No one would find me for a long time, probably. Why wouldn't he shoot me now? But he didn't.

I ran as fast as I could and got back to a familiar crack house. Of course, I was still crying and trying to tell my story. I was dirty and my clothes were ragged and torn. *I've got to have a hit. I've got to have a hit.* I didn't have any money, but someone felt sorry for me and gave me a $3 hit so I could calm down for a few minutes. All that did was make me crave more. I begged and begged and finally realized I'd have to get back out there and do another trick to have enough to buy a hit.

Within an hour, I had gone to the apartment of a woman I knew. She let me take a shower and gave me some clean clothes. I was back on the street. *I've got to have another hit. I've just been through this awful thing and I deserve a hit. Soon as I get a hit, I'll be OK.*

That's what I was thinking. I didn't think about almost losing my life. I didn't think, *I'll call Mom and tell her I want to check into a program and get cleaned up again.* I didn't think, *I can't do this anymore.* All I could think was that I had to make some more money so I could get some more crack.

The power of addiction is so strong that I could convince myself I could go through anything if I just had enough drugs. Even having a gun held to my head and facing the real possibility of being blown away didn't make me realize how far gone I was.

After having such a terrifying experience, though, I tended to stay closer to familiar areas. I hooked up with Calvin, a dope dealer, and started doing some things for him. Calvin rented a few apartments together in one place and he pimped several girls there. Since I knew almost everyone, I was able to introduce him to some more girls and get them set up with him.

Sometimes I'd do errands for him, and frequently he would have me sit out on the front stoop and watch for the cops. Everyone knew this place was full of drug dealers, and occasionally they'd come and raid the whole place. My job was to watch out and warn everyone if I saw anything that looked like trouble.

So I had about six months of pretty good living. Calvin gave me a place to stay and plenty of crack in exchange for bringing in the girls, doing his errands, and doing whatever else he needed.

One night, Calvin sent me out to the back courtyard to make sure the coast was clear. When I rounded the corner into the courtyard, cops were lying all over the ground and hidden behind cars in the parking lot. At least a dozen guns pointed right at me. It scared me to death. One of the officers put his finger to his lips in the shush signal and I froze right where I was. Calvin was only seconds behind me, and when he came into the courtyard, they pounced on him.

They searched both Calvin and me, but I was clean, amazingly enough. Calvin had drugs on him, and when they made him open the trunk of his car, it was loaded with drugs, money, and weapons. They let me go, but they took Calvin to jail. He ended up in prison, so I was out of a job and back to my own devices.

The next few years were the same story involving drinking, drugging, and surviving. We shared our drugs, drinking, and a multitude of problems. Then it was over.

Living with a man usually meant a one-room apartment, but sometimes it was a nicer place if he had a job and a paycheck. If I was with a man who went to work during the day, that was all the better. I could do my "work" during the day and have my own little stash of dope from my earnings. Then he would come in at night with drugs he had bought and we'd party, sleep, and the next day would be more of the same.

Darrell was a friend I lived with off and on but we didn't have sex. We did our drugs together, but we'd also sit up late at night having great conversations. We talked about our lives, wondering why things had turned out like they had. I talked about my life as an x-ray tech and about my son. I told him about my mother and brother and how my mother-in-law had adopted my son.

Darrell knew who I was and what I was, but he was still my friend. I could go out and do my hustling and prostitution and come back and smoke my dope there. I'd share whatever drugs I had with him and he'd share with me. But we'd talk. We had a relationship without the sexual nastiness of all my other relationships with men.

Sometimes I'd just say, "Darrell, I need a hug. Will you hug me?" Often he'd hold me in his arms and let me cry. He had other girls, but he never made sex an issue with us. I guess that's what made me feel so comfortable with him. He didn't judge me or condemn me. He didn't demand from me.

I felt safe with Darrell and safety on the street was hard to come by. I don't mean to be dramatic when I say this, but during those years in the early to mid-1990s I had several scrapes with death. When you live mostly on the street and the people you hang out with are all dopers and alcoholics, it isn't all Mr. Nice Guy.

One night I jumped in a car with a guy and we went to a parking lot. When we were through, he pulled a gun on me and wanted his money back. He just thought he could get what he wanted, threaten me, and I'd give him back his money. "I'm not paying you for this, you . . ." He called me a nasty name.

I grabbed the gun, not thinking. It was just a reaction. His hand was on it and my hand was on it. The gun was pointed toward me and we were fighting over it. I was kicking and fighting. My thumb got hooked somehow in between the handle and the hammer of the gun. When he yanked the gun back, my thumb ripped apart between my thumb and index finger. My thumb was just dangling there with blood spurting everywhere. The guy freaked out, pushed me out of the car, and drove off.

I took off running, holding my hand and bleeding like crazy. It was a long, deep, open gash. I could see the bone. I ran straight to Darrell's house and grabbed a dirty rag off the floor and wrapped it around my hand. I didn't know what to do.

Darrell panicked. He swore he was taking me to the emergency room, but I knew they'd test me and find drugs in my body, so I was determined not to go. All I wanted was a hit. If I could get a hit, I'd be OK. The blood finally stopped flowing. I knew I needed stitches, but I needed a hit more. If I lost my thumb, I just would. Darrell got me some dope and I made it through the night.

The next day, I went to a drugstore and stole some peroxide, bandages, and over-the-counter painkillers. From my time working in hospitals, I knew it was important to keep the wound clean. That was the best I could do. My injury healed in time with no infection and left a long scar. I know God healed me, but back then I just claimed to be "lucky."

When dangerous things happened to me, the immediate fear of death would overwhelm me. I would cry and beg for my life. The short-lived fear was quickly replaced by desperate craving. Facing death soon became nothing to me. I had guns pulled on me several times. I got beaten up and knocked in the head. I was tough enough that I usually fought back—and ended up getting a worse beating.

I was destroying myself physically, but I didn't care. So what if I needed stitches? I needed a hit more. I needed a drink more. I needed to be free to make some more money so I could get more drugs. I sure couldn't spend hours in an emergency room where I wouldn't have any dope.

I saw horrible things happen to other people too. Deaths from overdose, stabbings, and shootings. It was all so common.

One night Darrell, a friend named Stacy, and I were hanging out at Darrell's place. Stacy liked to shoot up powder cocaine, but she also liked to cook it up and smoke crack rock too. Stacy went in the bathroom and was putting on her tourniquet to do her thing. We didn't care. Didn't even notice much.

Suddenly Darrell and I heard a loud crash. We threw our pipes and crack under the couch. We thought the police were raiding us. We jumped up and ran to the back of the house. That's when we realized nobody was coming through the door. It wasn't a raid. Stacy had fallen and hit her head. She had obviously overdosed in the bathroom.

We pulled her out of the bathroom and laid her on the bedroom floor. I was shaking her, trying to wake her, talking to her. There was no response but at least she was breathing and had a heartbeat. She was bleeding profusely from the head injury. She started biting her tongue, so I was afraid she was having a seizure. Thankfully, what I had learned at the hospital kicked in. I grabbed a hairbrush and put it in her mouth. She had already bitten her tongue so hard that blood was squirting everywhere.

We were scared to death. *Do we call 911 and, when they come, get arrested for drugs? If she died, would we get blamed for her death?* The panic was staggering, stifling. I kept wiping her face with a cold rag and talking to her, begging her to open her eyes.

All of a sudden, the seizure ceased. She started breathing more normally. We carried her to bed and gave her sips of water. In a few hours, she was herself again and all three of us sat on the couch and laughed about being afraid the police were coming to arrest us. Stacy had a cut on her head, but, like all of us, she sure didn't want to go to the hospital and have to explain that.

Did the fear and shock of Stacy's crisis make any of us want to quit our crack or alcohol or go to rehab or call our folks and ask for help? No. Not even for a second. It was over.

When I wasn't in Darrell's apartment, I had several other favorite places to hang out. One was Phelan Park (known as Needle Park because of all the drug syringes usually found there) near a popular barbecue place in Birmingham. I would meet men in that park and then we'd go somewhere and I'd make my money. Then I'd go back to the park and wait to see who else might come to me.

I met John in that park. He had a house in the area but didn't have a car. He'd occasionally walk by on his way to a doctor's appointment or some other errand. Sometimes we'd sit in the park and talk. John was a large, muscular man, an ex-truck driver from Texas. I enjoyed our friendship and our conversations.

One night he invited me to his house. He was drinking, and I was doing crack. He didn't like crack, but he sure did like his drink. We slept together for the first and only time that night. At some point, I passed out.

The next morning I woke to find a well-dressed man standing over me shaking my shoulder. He told me I needed to get up and go into the kitchen. I had no idea who he was or what was happening.

When I got to the kitchen, John was sitting at the table with the gentleman too.

"John needs to tell you something," said the man.

"Janet, I'm so sorry. I have to tell you that I'm HIV-positive."

I was surprised, but I wasn't really alarmed.

I said, "Why didn't you tell me before?"

The bottom line was he didn't tell me because he didn't know how I would react. The truth is, it might not have mattered to me. John wanted to be with me, and I wanted the $40 he gave me for it. That was the most I'd made in a long time.

The social worker—that's who this man turned out to be—evidently just happened to come for a home visit that next morning. After we talked and John told me about being HIV-positive, the social worker wanted to know if I was going to press charges. Are you kidding? John and I continued to be friends. I figured he had shown me kindness and given me shelter when I needed it. He was hurting in another way. He was dying possibly.

I figured if I caught AIDS, so be it. Maybe that would kill me and I'd get out of this life sooner. That's just the way I looked at it. It didn't slow me down. Whatever will be will be. I couldn't care less. Not about me and not about anybody else. But God in His mercy protected me one more time.

This was in the mid-1990s and there wasn't as much education about HIV/AIDS as there is now. I never used any protection during all those years, and I didn't know anyone else who did. Sexually transmitted diseases were part of the life. Several times I had to go to the health department and be treated for STDs. As irresponsible as it sounds, I never knew who gave it to me, and I don't know how many people I passed it along to.

I think back now and see how sick and deceived and blind I was. No matter what happened that was upsetting for a little while, it was merely a bump in the road. As soon as the trauma passed, I was right back out there again, making my little bits of money for another hit.

The dangerous entanglements and close calls with death never ceased. In fact, they increased. One day I was walking along somewhere on Center Street and a car pulled up with three guys inside. "Hey, Janet, come on with us. We'll take care of you."

I had seen one of them before, a big guy who hung around at some of the dope dealers I did business with. I never dreamed he was the freak he turned out to be. The other two I'd never seen before.

They took me to a house and we went upstairs to a back bedroom. The one I was familiar with, obviously their leader, locked the door and said, "Get naked, Janet, and let's get busy."

"I need a hit first," I said. "I'll take care of you, but I want a hit first." He slapped me and said, "b—, I said get naked." I was pretty surprised.

"What are you doing? You don't have to slap me. I'll do my share and you do your share, and your share right now is giving me a hit." I was talking a lot tougher than I felt.

Big Boy looked me straight in the eye and said, "Well, I'm going to kill you, Janet. It may take a day or it may take two days, but you're not going to leave here." I saw evil in his eyes like I'd never seen before. He balled up his fist and hit me again and said, "Now, b—, get out of your clothes."

I knew he was serious, so I went into tough-girl mode. I didn't want them to think I was scared. I sure wasn't going to cry and beg for my life. *Hey, I'm a tough, old street woman and I'm going to handle it.* That was going to be my attitude, no matter how hard I was shaking on the inside.

I was used to people being a little weird and that wouldn't bother me at all. I'd been through countless really scary incidents, but I hadn't seen this situation developing. The guy I knew had never exhibited this kind of behavior. One guy obviously had some kind of untreated mental issue, and the other guy was going to follow the leader. But nothing had warned me before we got in this room that I shouldn't be around them.

Part of me wanted to wimp out, cry, and beg them not to hurt me, but I think that's exactly what they wanted me to do, so I put on my tough-girl face and it seemed to work.

I did whatever they demanded and it was violent, but I refused to show any alarm. All the time, I was scoping out the room. The door was to my right and it had double locks. I'd never have time to turn both locks and get out before they stopped me. There were a couple of large windows at the far end of the room. I had no idea how far from the ground they were or what was beneath them.

The one guy hadn't bothered me. He squatted over in the corner enjoying his dope by himself.

I played it cool and did what they wanted. I took the slaps and the nasty, vulgar language and abuse and didn't react. When the dope ran out, that was a problem. So Big Boy left to go get some more and left No. 2 in charge. "Lock the door, man, and keep her in here. Now's your chance."

Turns out No. 2 had evidently hidden a hit. As soon as Big Boy left, he was busy loading his crack pipe. I knew I didn't have anything to worry about with the one guy, so this was my chance. Naked as a jaybird and knowing this was do or die, I ran for the window and dove head first through the glass without a moment's pause. I smacked the ground hard, but I sensed that nothing was broken. I was bleeding from glass cuts, but I knew I couldn't waste any time. I jumped to my feet and made a run for it.

I had no idea which way to go. I took off running down the middle of the street, holding my chest, and screaming into the darkness of late night or early morning. Lights flashed on all down the street and I'm sure people were looking out their windows. Frantically, I pounded on the doors of a couple of houses, screaming "Please, please let me in. I just need some clothes. Please."

"Get out of here, white girl!"

At the next house, when I went to the door, a hand reached out and gave me a man's button-down shirt.

Somebody had called the cops. Never had I been so relieved. Clutching that shirt around me, I ran to them yelling, "I've been raped. I was smoking dope with these guys and they tortured me and told me I'd never make it out alive." My cuts were bleeding like crazy.

The cops took me to Cooper Green, the local charity hospital at that time. They treated my cuts and gave me some scrubs to put on. The whole time I'm thinking, *I need a hit, I just need a hit. I deserve a hit right now.* The craving was overwhelming.

Left alone in the exam room, I quietly opened the door and walked down the hall to the water fountain to get a drink. And I kept going. I trucked through the nearby Children's Hospital parking lot, through the UAB campus, and back to a crack house in Southside.

"Please, please, give me just a little hit. See, I'm hurt, and I need a hit." Somebody in there told me he'd give me a hit for a trick. As bad as I was hurting right then, I dropped to earn a $3 hit.

I'm OK. I'm OK. How quickly I stuffed down the terror I had felt only a few hours earlier. I was on my way again. *Hey, I'm outta that one.*

When you're addicted like I was, it doesn't matter what you go through. Once you're out of it, you forget it. You're OK and the crisis is history. All that matters is your next hit or drink. It was scary and horrible while my life was threatened or I was in pain, but once I survived it, it was over.

Even though I looked death in the face any number of times, I somehow thought I was invincible. How do people get trapped into believing that? How did I believe it? I'd just say, *Well, that was a close call, but it really wasn't that bad.* Then I'd charge back into that life and go deeper and darker.

No big deal.

Chapter 13

TRUE FRIENDS

Women friends on the street were few, but friends who knew the truth and helped me anyway were really rare. Carole, the weekend supervisor I reconnected with at Hannah Home, is one of the dearest friends God ever gave me.

Carole lived just a few blocks from where I hung out in Southside. A few months after I left Hannah Home, I ran into her in the neighborhood and she asked me to come to her house. I was hungry and that was my main reason for going home with her. I figured she would give me something to eat.

I was right. She fed me and let me take a shower. She prayed and played some Christian music. Her demeanor was so soft and sweet and caring. You remember, Carole had lived a life similar to mine. I recognized her when I went to Hannah Home and knew she was like me. But that's just it. She wasn't like me. She used to be, but she had become a Christian, and Jesus had changed her heart completely.

"Janet, what are you doing? Why are you out here like this?" She said that Jesus had changed her and He would do the same for me. I told her it was too late. I couldn't stop. I'd tried, but it hadn't worked.

I didn't steal from her that first visit. But on my second or third visit, I began stealing from Carole. I took several small things, including her son's watch, and pawned them all for dope money. Sometimes I'd tell Carole that I needed money for a particular thing and she would give me money. I'd always use the money for drugs, and I'm sure I wasn't fooling her.

After a while, if I told Carole I needed something, she would take me to the store and buy it for me. Then she'd leave me and go on to do other errands. I'd walk down the street with my bag. When she was out of sight, I'd go back into the store and get a refund.

Carole saw our friendship as a way to show Jesus to me, and I saw it as a way to use her. Even though Carole knew what I was doing, she still offered her friendship. Sometimes we'd sit on the front porch and talk and not even go inside the house, which meant I didn't have the opportunity to steal from her. No matter what, her compassion for me never changed.

I know now that Carole was showing me the compassion of Christ. The Bible says if someone wants your coat, give your cloak too. That's what Carole did. She tried to tell me why she was doing all these things, but all I thought about was how much dope I could buy with the money I'd get from stealing and selling her jewelry.

Carole prayed for me for many, many years. Sometimes I was so ashamed, I wouldn't go around her. Then when I was desperate I'd go and say, "Carole, I need something to eat and maybe a shower. Is that OK?" Every time she would take me in, give me food, a shower, and clean clothes. Sometimes I'd wonder how she would react to me after I'd taken advantage of her so many times, but she was always the same.

Carole invited me to go with her to Grace and Truth Church. That's where I actually met Kathy Campbell, the young woman I had seen many times in the past driving around the green apartments. I knew she lived in the area and visited some people in one of the apartments. I recognized Kathy immediately. She welcomed me to Grace and Truth, as did everyone else, including the pastor, Steve Longnecker.

During these first few months back on the street, one day I was not feeling well. I was cramping and aching in my lower abdomen. Because of many things in my lifestyle, I didn't have regular periods, so I didn't realize that I was pregnant and that I was having a miscarriage.

As the pain grew worse, I went into a deserted crack house and lay down on a filthy mattress. The house was abandoned but I knew a secret entrance to it and from time to time it was my refuge. I still didn't know what was happening, but the pain was intense.

The specific details about this incident are a little fuzzy now, but I think Kathy was either running or walking in the neighborhood and heard me moaning. Realizing someone was in trouble, she called the police and they called an ambulance.

I was taken to Cooper Green for treatment, but the next day I was back on the street. Once again, emptiness engulfed me. In my twisted mind, I was mad at God for letting me have a miscarriage, but I was also mad at Him for letting me get pregnant again. That's how messed up I was.

When I think of Carole's and Kathy's faithful love for Jesus and for me, it brings tears of gratitude. Since my life has changed, I want to treat others as they treated me. Praise God for His forgiveness demonstrated through Carole, Kathy, and others He placed in my life in those years of darkness.

Many years later, Carole, Kathy, and Grace and Truth Church would be extremely important in my recovery. Praise God they didn't give up on me! Kathy is now in heaven and one day I'll see her again.

Chapter 14

TOM

After two failed marriages and a string of other men, you'd think that hooking up with a man would be the last thing I'd want. I'm certainly not counting as serious my frequent "dates" that were simply about making money to buy drugs. As much as I'd been hurt and had hurt other people, I still had the fairy-tale notion that somewhere, sometime I would meet my Prince Charming and walk off into the land of happily ever after.

That's when I met Tom. We had a lot in common. Both of us were desperate for crack and would do just about anything to get it. But other than our shared addiction, I was immediately attracted to Tom. He was medium height and really thin with deep-set brown eyes, dark hair and skin. Even then, he didn't have much hair on top, but he frequently wore what grew from the sides in a ponytail.

My heart was drawn to him and I knew he responded in the same way. I felt something for Tom that I hadn't felt for any man in a long time.

Tom was a "booster" and I became his partner in crime. This is how it worked: Tom would open a small bank account and get some counterchecks. Then he would go to a store and buy stuff and write a check. This was before businesses had ways of verifying your check and also before they started requiring a receipt with returned merchandise. Later that same day or maybe the next day, he would return whatever he had purchased, say he decided he didn't need it, and get cash back. Sometimes he would buy things, go down the street, change shirts, and walk right back in and get his "refund." Other times he would wait until a new cashier came on duty. But he'd always walk out with the money.

Tom was an expert at this game and he taught me well. We were a great team. One shop-and-return situation was a fairly easy way to get enough money to buy crack for a whole day. We'd go somewhere and smoke it up and start the same game again the next day.

Tom did odd jobs like painting and sheet-rocking on construction or remodeling sites. I started going on jobs with him and his boss would pay me to pick up shingles or hold the sheetrock and things like that. So we were in the money. Best of all, we'd both get paid cash at the end of the day. We'd rent a motel room and buy enough dope to last the night. Sometimes we'd just go into the basement of a building and stay there all night, smoking our crack and sleeping a little—and the usual partying of course.

For a long time, I was stuck in a cycle with Tom. He demanded that I be with him every minute of the day. He knew when we met that I was a prostitute, but, now that I was his girl, he didn't want me out of his sight. If I tried to leave or go anywhere without him, he'd get violent. He'd pull my hair, slap me around, and call me horrible names.

But the next day, he'd be back, saying he was sorry and he'd never do it again. He'd tell me he loved me. I'd be crying and upset. We'd make up, and the cycle would start all over again. I wanted to be with Tom and wanted to believe him. It usually helped that he would have enough money to buy our dope when I didn't have any.

Tom had a lawyer friend named Ted Pearson. Ted was always available to help Tom get out of jail or go to hearings with him. Meeting Ted was definitely a turning point in my life, although I didn't know it at that time, and nothing changed immediately.

Ted is not just someone who talks about being a Christian. He puts his faith into action every day. I met him those many years ago, and he's still a strong influence in my life today. Tom and I took advantage of Ted for a long time. He would let us work off Tom's legal fees by doing odd jobs around his house. His wife,

Karen, would usually invite us to eat with them. I was constantly hungry but rarely ate anything nutritious, so I really enjoyed sitting down to a big table of home-cooked food. Believe it or not, Tom and I often repaid their kindness by stealing something from their house that we could sell at a pawn shop for drug money.

Ted would let us take his van to buy supplies for whatever job we were doing. More than once, we'd drive somewhere to buy drugs and stay gone a couple of days. Ted would find us, give us a good tongue lashing, and take the van back. But when we needed help the next time, Ted was always willing to give us another chance. His grace, like God's grace, seemed inexhaustible.

Why would Ted do all this for us when we did nothing but take advantage of him? He had—and still has—a ministry to homeless drug addicts and alcoholics. He truly believed that God could change us, and he was willing to hang in there with us until that happened. For me, that change would still be years away, but I am eternally grateful for Ted's investment in my life. Without his friendship and example, where would I be today?

Ted is a member of Third Presbyterian Church in downtown Birmingham. He'd invite us to church and sometimes we'd go, especially when we wanted something from him or thought we needed to make up for doing something terrible. Ted continues to bring homeless street people, addicts, and parolees to church. He always has visitors with him on Sundays and Wednesday nights. At Third Presbyterian, it doesn't matter what you wear or where you've been. You're always welcome.

Tom and I were hired to do some painting and repairs at the church, so Ted got us a room in the nearby Hawthorne Suites. He bought us groceries and let us use his van to get back and forth to the job. We'd also drive to areas where we weren't known and panhandle. We'd tell people we were on our way to Atlanta and didn't have enough gas to get there. *We just lost our jobs and could you help us a little?* Then we'd take that money and Ted's van and go buy our dope for the night.

I got in touch with Mother and told her about Tom. Told her I was in love and we both were working and living in the Hawthorne

Suites and doing well. I know she hoped in her heart that I'd finally changed. She visited us there several times and would always bring things to us. She wanted my life to straighten out and tried to be supportive in every way possible.

Sometimes I think about all those other girls I knew out there using and abusing and how much their families suffered. Mothers always seem to hold out hope. Even in the times that she said I couldn't come back home, I knew when I would call her and tell her I was with someone and doing better, she still hoped it was true.

We moved from working on the church to doing some of the same kind of work for a guy named Jerry. We'd been given many chances but still managed to blow things with Ted. Jerry was our next victim. He wanted to remodel the basement of a rental house he owned in Southside, so he let us live there while we transformed that unfinished basement into a beautiful one-bedroom apartment.

The other big news at this time was that I was pregnant again. This was definitely Tom's baby. Living in the basement and expecting a child gave both of us a little lift in a way. We talked about cleaning up our lives and quitting the dope. We could have a regular life, we told ourselves. But as much as we talked, when we got money, we went straight to the dope man. Yet, this was a more normal life than we'd ever had. We had a good, clean place to live and groceries in the refrigerator.

Somebody came by our house and invited us to visit Glen Iris Baptist Church. We didn't have dress clothes, but they welcomed us in what we had. A lady named Mrs. Aaron took a liking to me and wanted to help me. We'd go to breakfast together and talk about spiritual things and then she'd take me home. I even got baptized at Glen Iris, and we went to church almost every Sunday for several weeks.

I remember definitely seeing something I admired and wanted in these people at church. They seemed to have joy and peace that I didn't know was possible, the same qualities I'd seen in the people who worked at Hannah Home. I thought being baptized would be like waking from a dream of some kind. I expected to rise up from those waters and my life would be different on the outside even though I'd made no change on the inside. I still wanted to live in sin with Tom, drink, do drugs, and live that other life, and then on Sunday go to church and pretend I had changed. My fake life didn't satisfy and the pretending didn't change me. I was the same Janet. It wasn't long until I didn't want to fake it anymore and we quit church.

I told Mother I was pregnant. I gave her the line about straightening up. "Tom and I are in love and we're doing well." Of course, in the meantime, Tom and I were having screaming and cursing fights, and sometimes even physical fights. I fooled everyone for a while and sometimes even fooled myself into thinking things could be different.

Even though I was mistreated and abused, I wasn't alone, and I settled for that. In my heart, I believed I didn't deserve to be treated any better. At least sometimes Tom would hold me and tell me he loved me. Maybe I thought the good times made up for the bad ones. The truth is that I often abused Tom and others. Although I was often a victim, I was the one who abused too.

I was not always faithful to Tom, either. I would leave and be with someone else to get money for drugs and then come back and lie to him about where I'd been. I'd cheat on him and lie to him and he would hurt me by beating me.

Jerry rented the upstairs of the house to a family, and they could hear us fighting and yelling. Also, we always had a string of people who came by to hang out and do their drugs in our apartment. Finally, the upstairs tenants complained enough that Jerry told us to leave.

Once again we called Ted. Why would Ted even speak to us, much less help us? But, bless God, he did. He set us up in a little trailer in Irondale, a nearby suburb of Birmingham, that belonged to his son. The trailer needed gutting and remodeling, so he let us stay there and do the work. Ted even bought us an old Toyota Corolla so we could go to places to buy supplies.

While I was pregnant, both Tom and I spent time in jail on probation violations. One or the other of us would spend a few days in jail and then we'd get out and go back to the trailer and work some more.

Tom decided he wanted us to get married and to really try to quit the dope and get straight. We would promise not to hurt each other, and I wouldn't prostitute any more. We were going to be together forever and have this baby and raise it right. I agreed with all that and really wanted it to happen. Happily ever after was what I had always wanted.

We told Mother we were going to get married. She brought some things for us and even helped me plant some hostas and make a little rock garden outside the trailer. We also set out some tomato plants. We even took in a stray cat. We thought that we looked like the ordinary couple expecting their first baby.

Some people from Irondale Baptist Church came through with a produce truck. They'd drive through a neighborhood and offer their produce and then tell people about the church and invite them to attend. So we went to church, told them we were married and expecting a baby, and even joined a Sunday School class filled with couples about our age. We gave them the same story we'd used before. We had fallen on hard times and we were trying to get back on our feet. We'd lost everything, but we'd be OK.

Those kind people took us in. More correctly, I guess you could say we took them in. They never seemed to suspect anything about our drug problems. At least, not at that time. They gave us furniture, including a bedroom suite, living room suite, and a kitchen table. They brought us produce from their gardens and bags of groceries from the store.

Of course, the part about getting married never happened. For one thing, I had never been divorced from Dean. Tom occasionally would ask Ted to find out what could be done to locate Dean and file divorce papers. The truth was, although I was emotionally tied to Tom and we had been together off and on for several years, I know now that I didn't want to marry him. The good times were good, but Tom was violent so much of the time that I was often afraid of him. I never pushed Ted to follow through with the divorce. In fact, that didn't happen until several years later.

Even though Tom and I separated several times through the years, I often thought Tom was all I had and if I didn't stay with him, I had no one. I believe I thought I couldn't have a different kind of relationship than one of abuse and control. I heard someone say that many women think having any man is better than having no man. That's how I must have felt in those days. I know we were caught up in a spider web of codependency, but at that time I felt helpless to do anything about it.

Our life together was a network of lies. As soon as Tom got a payday, we'd buy our dope and a 12-pack of beer. *We'll do it just this once. One more time*, we'd tell ourselves. At one point, Tom decided that since I was pregnant I didn't need to be drinking and using crack. That made me furious. "If you think you're going to sit right here in front of me and smoke crack and say I can't have any, you've got another think coming!"

Ted would come by now and then to see how we were doing. He had bought enough supplies to see the job through and the tools to do it. "Where's the saw I bought?" He knew the answer before he asked the question. We'd taken the saw to the pawn shop for dope money. He went and bought the tools back.

A few times people from the church came by and we'd be inside smoking crack and wouldn't answer the door. We were just lying and gaming, not showing up for church and not being honest with Ted or anybody else.

Once we were fighting and Tom threw something at me and hit me in the stomach. "What are you doing? Are you trying to kill this baby?" Our fight got more violent. He wrestled me to the floor and choked me until I couldn't breathe. But while I was blaming Tom for harming the baby, what was I doing? Drinking, smoking crack and regular cigarettes, and everything else I wanted to do.

The people at church gave us a surprise baby shower at the home of one of the ladies. They gave us beautiful gifts. When the shower was over, I went straight to the stores and returned many of them for money to buy drugs for that day. I never let those people know any other life than the one they saw on the outside, but what I really lived was very different.

Chapter 15

BRANDON

Brandon was born June 10, 1998—a beautiful little boy. Just seeing that sweet face inspired me once again to truly want life to be different. I was 39 years old, and I decided I wanted to try to be a mother.

One night after I got home from the hospital with Brandon, Tom and I sat down to eat supper and I said something he objected to. I was holding Brandon and Tom picked up his plate of food and threw it at me. Our relationship all along had been violent at times and I began to be afraid he might hurt Brandon. The plate-throwing incident made me decide to leave Tom and go back to my mother's house.

So I called Mom and asked her if I could come home and bring Brandon with me. She agreed. I know she probably wanted to refuse, but she said I could come home.

Everything was going well until I went for my six-week checkup with the doctor. Mom was taking me to the doctor and Brandon was in his car seat. Another vehicle, driven by a teenage boy, pulled over in front of my mother's car and we had a wreck. No one was hurt. It seemed to take forever for the police to come and then even longer for them to question all of us and permit us to leave.

Although the car was drivable, Mom was extremely upset and crying and by then Brandon was hungry. I told Mom I really needed to go to this appointment, so she drove home with Brandon and I called a friend to come and take me to the doctor's office.

She dropped me off at the office, but I never even went in for the appointment. As soon as she was out of sight, I cut across the hospital parking lot and ran several blocks to one of my usual dope men. I spent the $30 in my pocket on crack. I didn't go home for more than a week. My week was spent running around the area, panhandling, prostituting, and getting high. I didn't have any clothes to change into or a place to take a bath or brush my teeth. I didn't call to check in with my mother or to ask about Brandon. The only thing on my mind was where I could get another hit.

About ten days after the wreck, I showed up at my mother's house. One more time I'd let her down in a big way. I walked into her house and saw the pain and disappointment on her face. I can't even imagine what she was thinking. She wouldn't speak to me for several days, but she didn't tell me to get out. After all, we had Brandon to think about now.

I remember holding Brandon in my arms and thinking, *I just can't do this. I love him and he needs me, but I can't do it*. I hadn't seen Tom since soon after Brandon was born. He'd gone to my mother's house a couple of times and given her money to give me. Mom didn't like Tom because in her mind my addiction was his fault. I know it's easier to blame someone other than your own flesh and blood, and that's what she did.

We got an insurance settlement for the car wreck and I ended up with $800. Boy, that seemed like a lot of money, but I had a dilemma. Mom was mad at me, I was saddled with a baby, and I didn't have a car. So I called Tom and told him I had some money. That's all it took to bring him running. We went straight to a crack house and took Brandon with us. Tom and I sat in one room and smoked our dope and left Brandon in his car seat in another room.

Every now and then I'd go change his diaper or prop a bottle or give him a pacifier. I had some baby formula in cans and I would rinse out a bottle and refill it. I never picked him up or held him. I just wanted him to be quiet and let me do my business—and that didn't include taking care of a baby.

After several days, I went to my mother's house to get some clothes and told her I was going to stay with Tom in the trailer. She begged me not to. She wanted me to come back and bring

Brandon. "No, I love Tom and he loves me and we're going to work it out." I was high while I was having this conversation with her.

So Tom and I took Brandon to the trailer. Tom had opened a bank account so he could get some counter checks. That night we went all around town writing checks and getting cash. Brandon was in the car seat all night, riding and sleeping. We got our dope and went home to smoke and drink for the next two or three days.

I remember being so doped up and needing to crash. During the night, Brandon was crying and hungry. Tom wouldn't get up. I got up and fixed a bottle and was sitting with Brandon in my lap. I dozed off and he rolled off onto the floor and under the couch. I was out cold. I woke up to hear him crying. I have no idea how long he had been under the couch.

I'll never forget how awful I felt. I was high and passed out and totally neglecting my baby. I wish that had been the extent of my neglect, but many times after that we would be in the dope houses for a couple of days and Brandon would be there in his car seat. How many times did he go hungry or remain wet while no one even picked him up or fed him? I'm so ashamed now about how I neglected Brandon.

Tom and I were boosting to make our dope money, and also panhandling. We still had the car Ted had given us, so we looked like a family. "Hey, can you help me? Just need a little gas to get back home. Having a hard time, you know. Thank you for your help."

One night we got pulled over by the police for a traffic violation and I had some outstanding warrants, so I was arrested. Tom took Brandon home and I went to jail for a few days. I can't even imagine how he neglected Brandon while I was gone. But, hey, I was neglecting him, too, so how could I say anything to Tom?

During the short time I was living with Mother, Brandon was cared for, but when it was just me and Tom, he was badly neglected. He breathed the secondhand smoke and wore dirty clothes and went hungry. I was putting him at risk in all kinds of ways, but the only thing that was important to me was dope and drink.

I guess it goes without saying that we weren't going to church anymore. Fact is, being around people who loved God just wasn't on our list of priorities. Crack was at the top, and that's all we thought about.

The car Ted had given us wore out and we abandoned it on the side of the road. Ted finally got tired of our deception and told us we needed to leave the trailer. I know he still wanted to help us, but we had stolen and lied to him and there was no end to it. He was totally exasperated.

One day Tom and I were panhandling in Phelan Park and a complaint was made to the police, so they came and arrested both of us. I sure didn't want to call my mother again, so the cops told me Brandon would go into foster care. Tom only served a few days, but another charge showed up on me and I had to stay a few days longer.

When I got out of jail, did I rush to find out about my baby, where he was, and what was happening to him? No way. I considered foster care a free babysitter, so I lived it up.

When I finally did try to find out where he was, the social workers didn't immediately give me the information I wanted. I screamed and cursed and ranted. "How dare you keep me away from my baby? I'll show you a thing or two!"

I called Ted and told him what was happening. As always, Ted went right to work to help me. He found out that the judge had ordered me to psychological counseling, drug treatment, and a lot more stuff that I had no intention of doing. In order for me to get Brandon back, I'd need to have a job and a stable home.

Tom and I went back to the trailer and cleaned it up a bit, but we were still doing all the wrong things. Brandon was still in foster care. One day, there was a knock on the door and when I opened it, there was a caseworker standing there. She'd come to do a home visit to determine if Brandon could be returned to us.

I lied to the caseworker and made excuses upon excuses. I was a smart aleck to her. I told her I was appalled that they would come and investigate me. "Hey, there's nothing wrong with me. You're just trying to trump up some reason to take my baby away for good. Just get outta my house and don't come back!" What I actually said was probably a lot more colorful. I was determined to fight back and justify the life I was living. I was so offended that anyone would challenge me.

Ted took me to the psychologist, as ordered by the judge. I lied about everything. I was allowed to do outpatient drug treatment, and Ted arranged for me to have supervised visits with Brandon. For those visits, I'd clean up and go downtown where I'd meet the social worker. She would stay in the room with me, and I'd pretend to be the loving, caring mother.

Then I'd leave there and go prostitute to get money for more drugs. A never-ending cycle. In my warped thinking, I deserved to do anything I wanted because, poor me, nothing ever worked out right. Why try anymore? Nobody really cared, so I wasn't going to care either.

I never got my little boy back. The court took away my parental rights, and they had every reason to do so. As I write this, I know nothing about where he is or what his life is like. I trust that God has provided him with a safe home and a loving family.

Once again, I felt that everybody had done me wrong. How dare they take my child away and tell me to sign over my parental rights? I cursed them all. I was angry and bitter. Look what they'd done to me again is what I thought then.

I'd love to see Brandon now, not to take him away and not to interfere in his life, but just to see him. I'd like to ask his forgiveness and tell him I love him. I know that God has taken care of Brandon. I have to believe that in my heart.

Just yesterday, I was on the street in downtown Birmingham during my lunch break. A man sitting on the street asked me for some money. Said it was for food, that he was hungry. I only had a dollar and some change, but I gave it to him.

As I was handing him the money, another man came along with a baby in a stroller. He also asked if I could give him some money. I told him I'd just given all the cash I had to the other man. He pushed the stroller into the intersection and went up to a car stopped at a traffic light. I saw the people in the car hand him some money. I'm making a judgment, but I'm pretty sure he was begging money for drugs, not for food, just as I had so many times.

I thought of all the times I'd used Brandon to get money. I even sold my welfare vouchers (WIC) to get money for drugs. Then I'd go in a store and steal formula.

Yes, I knew what that man was doing. I saw myself in him.

With Brandon gone, I started taking even more risks. Why not? Although I hadn't taken care of him, losing him was just one more validation of my lack of worth.

One night I got in a car with a man who said he wanted me to go to his brother's house. We drove and drove. Gravel road, dirt road. I don't even know where we were or how we got there. By then, I was getting a little concerned. He stopped the car, and there wasn't even a place to pull over. He just started attacking me while screaming obscenities.

I wondered if he was going to kill me out there in the middle of nowhere. Somehow I opened the car door and literally fell out on the road. Before he could crawl over and get me, I jumped to my feet and started running. Tripping, limbs hitting my face, running like crazy. I couldn't see and had no idea if I would ever come out near civilization, but I knew I had to keep going.

Finally, I just lay down on the dirt, totally exhausted. I tried to slow my breathing. I didn't know if he was close or not. In a little while, I heard a car motor start and I knew he was gone.

I remember thinking, *Oh God, help me. I don't want to die. I don't want to die.*

Now, there had certainly been many times when I'd prayed *to* die—when someone put a gun to my head or a knife on my neck—but this time I was praying to live.

I've got to get out of here, I told myself. *I've got to get help.* My clothes were ragged and torn and my face and arms were bleeding from the briars and limbs. *I can't believe this has happened. I need a hit so bad. This is too much to handle.* See, no matter what happened, my answer was a hit or a drink.

I finally made it to a dirt road and stopped to catch my breath. As I was standing there wondering which way to go, the sounds of the woods were all around me. Suddenly I was slammed to the ground. It was him. He pinned me to the ground and hit me again and again with both fists. I gave up. I had no fight left in me. He raped me and then walked to his car and left.

I lay there on the ground for a long time, my tears mixing with the dirt and blood. I was hurting so bad I didn't know if I could walk or not. When I gathered the strength to stand, I stumbled to where the dirt road intersected a paved road, and I waved frantically at a couple of passing cars, but they didn't stop. A truck finally stopped. I stumbled up to the window and told the truck driver I needed a ride to Birmingham. I must have been a tragic sight, but he was kind. He dropped me off near the interstate and gave me $5, which I took to the nearest crack house.

I told everybody there what had happened, trying to get them to feel sorry for me and give me some free dope. No luck. I scrounged around in a closet at that house and found some clothes, washed up a bit, and went out and started tricking again that same night. Now, I can hardly believe it. No matter what happened to me, nothing was bad enough to make me quit the dope. Nothing was more important. No matter how bad it was, I still wanted that hit or that swig from a bottle.

Even when I survived a crisis, I didn't feel that I got any breaks. I thought that I wasn't one of those ladies with a drug problem that had a sugar daddy to help me. I wasn't one that lived in the affluent neighborhood and drove up in my fancy car to get my dope for the weekend and then back to my fine house to smoke it. I always had to scratch and dig for it.

So I became a Jack-of-all-trades throughout my years of abusing because I learned if I couldn't get a hit one way, there was always another perverted way. It didn't matter what I did or how bad it might seem to anyone with any sense of morals, I would do it. I was living only for my next high or my next drink, and getting it was worth doing whatever it took.

Every now and then somebody would ask me, "Why don't you get off the crack and make something of yourself? You can do better." My reply was always the same: "Hey, I can't start over. How can I start over? It's too late."

I'd lost it all. *Where would I go?*

Tom was frequently in jail for forged checks, probation violations, and things like that, but we'd be together now and then too. He always seemed to look for me, and I knew I could depend on him to share whatever drugs he had.

The cops that patrolled the area knew me. One night I was hanging around Phelan Park and I'd just gotten out of jail that day after serving about three weeks. I had done some tricks and bought a little crack and I had some crack stems hidden.

One of the cops I knew came along and said, "Janet, I believe there's an outstanding warrant on you." He said he was going to have to take me in. "Do you have anything on you, Janet? You're going to be charged with a probation violation, but if you go in with anything on you, it's going to be worse."

He already had me handcuffed. In a moment when his back was turned, I was able to get rid of those stems, dropping them down to the ground from where I had them hidden inside my clothing. I went on to jail.

In all, between my first arrest and the time I got straight, I had been in jail on 17 charges, all for misdemeanors like stealing, writing a bad check, and traffic violations. I never had a felony charge, like drug possession. That's certainly not to say I didn't deserve to be charged with more. I'd play both sides of the street, whichever would get me a hit at the time.

By now I had a reputation for being willing to do anything. As long as I got a hit, it didn't matter. Nothing mattered much. The sun coming up or the sun going down. A cold or a backache or a hunger pang. It really didn't make any difference. Normal things, you know, like my hair needing washing or how nice it would be to put on some makeup or have a morning cup of coffee. Normal things left my mind.

My mother or my brother or my children—thoughts of them rarely entered my mind. Life as I once knew it years ago was all gone. Crack, alcohol, and prostitution were my life now. I lived for those things and nothing else.

Chapter 16

THE BEGINNING OF THE END

At the age of 41, I was pregnant again. Well, no big deal, I decided. I'd had those previous pregnancies, and I was determined that this one wasn't going to slow me down. The other times, I had gone to Hannah Home, home to Mother, signed adoption papers, lost my rights, and walked away. This time I was just going to let it happen as it happened and not think about it.

I had no prenatal care and didn't plan on getting any. When the time came, I told myself, I'd go have that baby, the state would take the baby, and I'd be right back on the street.

The surprising thing is, most of the men didn't care that I was pregnant. Just so they got what they wanted, they were fine with it. One drug dealer refused to sell to me. He said he wouldn't sell drugs to a pregnant woman, but he was the only one.

As I got bigger, I had to find more clothes. My usual way was to look in dumpsters or in bags thrown out on the street. Whatever I had, I wore for months, until it completely wore out or had been torn off me. Sometimes I'd steal clothes from a self-service laundry. Now, being pregnant, I looked for larger, baggier clothes that I could tie up with a string or belt.

As my pregnancy began to show, people started asking me about when I was going to the doctor or when I was going to stop getting high and start caring about the baby. Even lifelong addicts were encouraging me to quit until the baby was born. I got sick of hearing it. I got tired of people bothering me. They just wanted to get in my business and put me down. They didn't care about me.

I knew a woman named Dee who would occasionally let me come in her apartment and take a shower and wash my clothes. Of course, I had to go make money for some dope and bring her a hit to pay for those privileges.

Several times during the pregnancy, Dee let me go in a back room and crash. I was so tired. Exhausted. Nowhere else to go. As this pregnancy progressed, I couldn't deny that it was more difficult than previous pregnancies. My age, lack of medical care and nutritious food, and the stress of my lifestyle were wearing me down.

Sometimes in the crack houses, even though I'd be tired, it would take a while to go to sleep. I'd close my eyes and just rest. But I could hear them. "Look, man, that's Janet over there. Yeah, she's pregnant. Yeah, she's real bad off. She's killing that kid."

I'd lie there and pretend not to hear, but it hurt. It really hurt. *How long can I do this? When am I just going to die?* I'd turn my face to the wall and silently cry. In my mind, I cursed God and myself and the whole world.

Sometimes I'd wish I could go back. I'd remember the days when I had a job as an x-ray tech. I'd think about the children I had lost. My mom and the smell of her house. The person I used to be. And I'd wonder what had happened. *Why did this happen to me?*

I always thought in those terms, that all the bad things "happened" to me. I didn't for a minute think that I was personally and totally responsible for making choices that led to the circumstances in my life. Oh no.

I sure felt sorry for myself a lot and blamed a lot of other people for my life. *People did me wrong. God sure did me wrong. But don't think about them, Janet. They don't care about you.* I'd stuff it all down, then get up and go on. I thought nobody was as desperate as me.

Sometimes I'd go looking for Tom or he'd come looking for me. I kind of think we were all each other had, as weird and pitiful as it was. We'd hang out for a day or two and share our dope and then we'd go our separate ways again.

One night, I was at Dee's and there were a lot of people there. I don't know how far along my pregnancy was, but I was big and my breasts were huge and every time I took a hit I would vomit or get the dry heaves. So I was glad to be at Dee's where the men could come to me and I'd do whatever they wanted right there in the back bedroom or the bathroom and I'd get my dope. I wasn't walking the streets or begging that night.

I had just done a trick with a guy and I sat down on the couch to enjoy my crack when my water broke. I went to the bathroom and saw that my clothes were soaked with mucous. I was furious. I cursed and ranted there in the bathroom where no one could hear me. Horrible language. *How can this happen tonight? Everything's going so well. I've got my men coming in and I've got my dope and I don't have to go out anywhere to get it.*

I cleaned up and went back to the living room. *Nobody needs to know this. They'll put me out if they know. They sure don't want the hassle of a baby being born here or the drama of an ambulance pulling up in front of the crack house.*

I lay down on my back with my feet up against the wall. I loaded my crack pipe and smoked it. Even this wasn't going to keep me from getting high. I tried to forget, and it felt good. But, of course, that good feeling was only temporary.

My stomach started tossing and turning and rumbling. *OK, I'm in labor, but I'm getting high. I've got several crack rocks left and I've got to figure out a way to keep doing this. Nobody will find out. I can hide this.*

I'd had plenty of physical pain in my life. I'd been beaten and raped and kicked and tied up. I'd had my hair pulled and my gut punched and my throat choked. I'd had cuts that took 20 or 30 stitches, and plenty of times I'd not gotten sewn up because I didn't want to stop getting high. This pain wasn't going to be any different. I could manage it, and I could keep getting high.

Which is exactly what I did even while I was having contractions. I determined to do whatever was necessary. No one had a clue that I was in labor.

Morning came and everyone was leaving. Most of them were out of money and probably the dope had run out by that time. Dee told me I'd have to leave. I was having deep contractions by this time. More painful and closer together. But I had such strong cravings, and that was all I could think about. My addiction over the years had grown to limits that could never be satisfied, and maybe my labor pains made the need even more intense.

I needed a fix. I walked around trying to find some way to get another hit. *Would they even let me in anywhere?* I wondered if anyone would even want me. Everybody knew I was nasty, homeless, toothless, and now 41 years old and pregnant. I felt lucky to turn a trick for a couple of dollars now. Something was better than nothing. I could at least get a bottle of wine for about a dollar. That would help for the moment.

But I didn't have a cent, so I knew I'd have to do something to get some money before I could get any more drugs. It was obvious by now that nobody was going to help me just because they felt sorry for me.

I made it down the hill to Phelan Park. I'd stop and hold on to one of those orange newspaper stands or a telephone pole until that powerful, agonizing contraction eased through me and the pain left my body.

By then it was daybreak on Saturday morning, November 11, 2000.

I begged $3 from the guy filling the newspaper stands. Got to the park and saw some of my wino buddies. We all would sleep together in basements on cold winter nights and share whatever food we found. We fought about who drank the most of the wine when we had only one bottle for all of us.

I've got to get this baby out of me. I don't want to go to the hospital. They'll keep me. They might even take me to jail because they'll find crack and alcohol in my bloodstream. In the baby too. I've got to figure something out. I've got to get another hit. I can't have this baby right now. I would squeeze and flow with the contraction and walk some more.

I ran into a guy I knew and did what he wanted for $5. *I've got to get some more money.*

I made it back up to Dee's and, with the $5 I'd made and the $3 from the newspaper boy, bought an $8 rock. I had my own stem. I sat down and put my legs straight out and took that hit. The pain was so severe I didn't know if I could keep from screaming out loud. I gritted what teeth I had and held it back.

When that hit was gone, I left and started down the hill again. I heard that familiar voice of Satan, *Go find a place to have this baby, wrap it up, and leave it. Go back to the dope house and hope they'll give you a hit because they'll feel sorry for you. Don't bother with a hospital. Somebody will find the baby and take care of it.*

I went across the street and around a restaurant to the dumpster in back, but I couldn't stay there. Too public. I headed on down to an abandoned house. *Well, maybe I can go down in the basement, have the baby, cut the cord, and nobody will hear me scream. I can do this. I can do this.*

But what if I bleed to death or the baby bleeds to death? Even as low as I was and as much as I didn't want this baby, I didn't want to kill it. I refused to listen to that voice, but I didn't know what to do. I was terrified. I knew I was going to have a baby right there on the street.

I went back to my wino friends across the street in the park. They were drunk. "Lay down over there, Janet, and we'll deliver that baby." They laughed and gave me a drink of their wine—a big gulp. I guess they realized then how desperate and terrified I was and they hollered for help. It was almost two o'clock in the afternoon. I'd been walking up and down the hill and around the park all day.

Just one more hit. Just one more hit. Please, please, just one more.

Chapter 17

DELIVERANCE DAY

Someone from a barbecue place called an ambulance. Even though it was a cool fall day, I wore only a T-shirt and a pair of black stretch pants. I didn't have shoes or underwear. My shoulder-length hair was thin, matted, and dirty. And the teeth I did have were either broken off or rotted out.

One more hit. Please, just one more hit.

The ambulance came and the EMTs put me on a stretcher. I was cursing and screaming at the top of my lungs. The urge to push was so great, and I knew this baby was on its way.

"It's coming! It's coming! Get this thing out of me!"

No telling how many men I'd been with since my last bath probably two weeks ago. I was nasty.

"Ma'am, please try to hold back! We're going to Cooper Green Hospital, and it's not far. Hold back!"

"Get this kid out of me!" All I wanted right now was another hit, and the quickest way was to get this over with and get back to the dope house.

"She's delivering!"

We skidded into the entrance of the ER at Cooper Green Mercy Hospital. Everyone was frantic, screaming instructions as they raced my gurney through the ER doors and down the hall straight to delivery.

When we got to the delivery room, all the medical people were rushing to get everything ready. They were telling me what to do, and I was cursing at the top of my lungs. "Hurry up and get it out!

Get it out! I don't want this thing! Get it out and let me out of here! I'm leaving and you can't make me stay!"

All that was in my mind was where I was going to get a hit. I didn't have any money, of course, but surely if I could make it back to Dee's, they would feel sorry for me. Just a little hit to help me.

I'm pushing. I'm pushing. "Get it out of me and I'm leaving!"

Everyone was screaming at this point. The nurses and doctors were trying to get me to cooperate and they were yelling instructions at each other. I was fighting them and screaming obscenities. The room was a den of noises and frenzy.

And then it happened.

A lacy net of beautiful, peaceful silence fell over the room. At least, it fell over me. I think the room went on in chaos, but I couldn't hear any of it. My inner soul got quiet and still. Completely serene. There was a Presence, Someone in the room that I couldn't see or touch, Someone reaching out to me.

The nurses and doctors kept moving around and doing their thing as the contractions came hard and fast, but I escaped into another world.

I felt the Presence, and I knew something was happening, but I couldn't quite understand what. Overwhelming peace wrapped its gentle arms around me. And then, in the depths of my spirit, I heard the voice.

When will you let Me love you?

I didn't know what to think. Maybe I should have been alarmed, but I felt totally comfortable and serene. I didn't know where the voice came from or who it was. I did know I was giving birth to a baby I didn't want. I knew I was homeless and destitute. But still the voice called to me.

When will you let Me love you, Janet?

I wanted to respond somehow, but all I could do was listen.

Aren't you tired, Janet? Let Me love you.

Yes, I was tired. Tired in my body and my mind and my spirit. I was trapped in a life of addiction, homelessness, and prostitution.

Let Me love you.

God! The Lord Jesus Christ was speaking to me!

By His Spirit speaking to my spirit, He made Himself known to me that day. Here I was: filthy, stinking, covered in sin and lies and deceit, covered in darkness. But the light of Jesus hit me. He told me He loved me.

God opened my eyes that day. He revealed truth so I could see and know Him. He played a picture of my life in my mind, a lifetime of sin. I saw the kids I'd given away, never wanting to be a mother. I saw the child I murdered through abortion and the miscarriage because of drugs and alcohol. The way I used to curse and hate my mom and dad. The way I lied and deceived so many people. My two unfaithful marriages. All the selfishness and hurt and pain I had caused so many people.

He let me look at all that. I felt ashamed and dirty and low, and I felt the pain of everything my life had been. I saw it all. It was real and ugly. All the sin and filthiness ripped through my heart.

When I didn't even think about God or think I needed Him, He shined his pure and holy light on my darkness and exposed it for what it was. Nasty, ugly, and sinful.

Lost. Lost. Lost.

In my spirit, I said, *Lord, it's too late for me. Look at all I've done.*

Right there on the delivery table, I began to sob. I was so ashamed of who I was and how I had never believed in Him or thought I needed Him. I remember saying in my spirit, *I'm so sorry, God. Please help me. Please forgive me.*

I knew He was saying, *Come to Me. I offer you life.*

Even as I was saying, *It's too late,* because I was convinced it was, God was saying, *Just believe. Just believe on Me. I'll give you a life you've never seen.*

And that's what I did that day. I believed. He forgave me then and there. He had loved me and had His hand on my life all along. That had to be true for me to have survived all those years, but I'd ignored Him.

I knew immediately that I was different. I felt new and really alive for the first time in my life. I felt His forgiveness wash over me and change me. Yes, although I didn't know the spiritual words to say, I had been cleansed and healed by the blood of Jesus.

My baby was born. "A beautiful little girl," the nurse said.

"Can I hold her?" They put her on top of me and I can't begin to tell you how much I loved her in that moment. Just an hour before, I'd been screaming about how I wanted to be rid of her, and now I knew I wanted nothing more than to raise this child.

I was concerned about what I might have done to her with the months of crack and alcohol and cigarettes, to say nothing of prostituting right up to the hour I went to the hospital. And the malnutrition and lack of prenatal care.

"Is she OK? Is she OK?" On first inspection, they couldn't find a thing wrong with her. They ran various tests over the next few days and found no problems. As I write this, my Brittany Anne is 12 years old and has never exhibited any problems that are typical for crack or alcohol babies. Praise God for His goodness!

So I had given birth to a sweet little baby girl, 7 pounds and 12 ounces, 20 inches long. But I had even more. Jesus Christ had come into my life and He had welcomed me into His kingdom.

Delivered!

Sometimes I say there were two deliveries on that November day. My little girl got her first life, and Jesus Christ gave me new life.

Delivered!

No regrets. No turning back.

Is it still hard to believe what He's done for me? I sure didn't deserve this miracle in my life, but, then, that's God's miracle for everyone, isn't it? We're sinners. We don't deserve anything, but God's love can cover all our sin. It's a truth I can't comprehend, but I know it's true.

More than a decade later, I'm still amazed, but God's presence in my life is just as real as it was that day in November 2000. From that first day, He began changing me into His image and fulfilling His purpose in me.

On that miraculous day, I was definitely plucked out of the muck and mire and placed on the Rock, the Solid Rock of Jesus

Christ. The craziness stopped that day. No, my life is definitely not perfect now and certainly I'm not perfect. The last 12-plus years have been a journey, and that journey will continue until I draw my last breath.

But I know without a tinge of doubt that there is nothing in my former life worth going back to. No high big enough or long enough, and no drug or drink or relationship of any kind that could snatch me out of His hands. When God told me on that delivery table that He offered me rest and life, He meant He wanted all of me. That's what I've given Him.

We serve a great and powerful God who can take us from darkness and put us into the blinding light of His love for eternity, forever with Him. The sins of yesterday can't haunt me and pull me back because I've been forgiven. I've been made new.

I'm not just an isolated one-in-a-million person. In some way, everyone is a Janet. We all sin, and sin is sin, no matter what it is. We all need Jesus. And, as much as we think our sin is too much, He is ready to wipe the slate clean. If my life stands for anything right now, it's to shout that message loud and clear. Jesus saves!

As powerful as my addictions were, the day God saved me, those cravings were taken away. I have never wanted drugs or alcohol since that moment. I know that doesn't happen for everyone. People tell me they're saved but they battle cravings every day. And some, of course, give in. I don't have an explanation for that. I simply know that God in His mercy took that desire away from me.

When I was taken to a hospital room, I took a shower and washed my hair. The warm water felt glorious as it washed over my tired and filthy body. I washed my T-shirt and black stretch pants in the sink and hung them up to dry.

One of the first times the nurse brought my baby into the room, she asked what her name was. I had no hesitation. *Brittany Anne.* During this entire pregnancy, never once had I thought about what I would name this baby, because, of course, I was not going to be concerned with anything, much less a name. In that moment, her name tumbled out of my mouth as if I'd planned it for months.

Every couple of hours they'd bring my baby girl to me and I'd hold her and feed her and cuddle with her. I was so in love with her. I couldn't even believe how I felt compared to only a few hours earlier when I'd come into the hospital cursing at her birth. I counted the minutes between times when the nurses brought her to me.

Remembering the Christian ladies who tried to help me before, I got the phone book and called the Hannah Home. When I was there a few years earlier, I wasn't ready to listen. I'd been polite, but I just went through the motions. I told the person at the Hannah Home that I wanted to come there and bring my baby. I wanted a chance to start life over and learn about God and how to take care of this baby.

I also called Kathy Campbell, my wonderful Christian friend who had helped me a number of times in the past, especially when I had the miscarriage. I had stayed with her before and had even stolen from her. From the time we met, I knew she cared for me and had continued to pray for me. She came to the hospital and brought a pretty diaper bag and a little pink teddy bear. We still have that bear.

Ted Pearson had tried for years to help me and Tom, so I also called him. Even after all the things I'd done to him, he and his wife came to see me and were happy to know that my life had been changed. They prayed with me. Ted and Karen Pearson are still my friends. Ted never gave up on me no matter how much I took advantage of him. I stole from him, lied to him, and manipulated him, but he still did everything he could to help me.

Every night in that hospital bed, I slept peacefully, and I still rest that way. Safe and peaceful, protected and loved. I have nothing to fear.

I hadn't heard back from Hannah Home when, a couple of days later, a nurse came in and told me I was being discharged.

"You're free to go."

"Go where?" I asked.

"Well, back home or wherever you live."

"I don't have a home." Now I'm not screaming or cursing. I'm calm and humble. "I don't have anywhere to go."

I told her I was a crack user and that I needed help and wanted help. "I want to keep my baby and raise her, but I need help. Please don't make me leave today. I'm trying to get into Hannah Home."

"Well, you're free to go. Is there someone you can stay with?"

"No, ma'am. Please don't make me go and take my baby until I find out if I can get into Hannah Home."

"Oh, you can go, but your baby is not going. Your baby is going into child custody. You were positive for cocaine and so was your baby. You won't be permitted to leave with your child."

I began to cry. It hadn't occurred to me—why didn't I think of that?—that I wouldn't be able to take Brittany with me. "Please don't let me lose my baby. I want her with me. I want to raise her. I want help. Please don't let me lose her. Please let me stay."

"These are the papers. They're final. You've been discharged."

I was crying and pleading. The head nurse and the doctor came in. I was telling them that I was homeless and I wanted to go somewhere and get some help, but I wanted to keep my baby. The doctor had mercy on me. "Well, we don't have to make a big deal over it. Let her stay another night. Ms. Gillispie, a social worker will talk with you tomorrow."

Relief flooded over me. I knew God was going to take care of me. Didn't He say all things are possible with Him? Oh yeah, I'm telling you, it's true.

Chapter 18

NO TURNING BACK

The next morning I got up and put on the clothes I'd washed out in the bathroom sink. I tied a knot in those black stretch pants where the belly used to be. I was ready. Fresh and clean.

The social worker came to talk with me about the drug test that was positive when I came in. I listened with an open heart. My attitude was far different than when I entered the hospital. I told the social worker that I'd had a troubled past and had done many wrong things, but now I wanted a chance to get straightened out and keep my baby. She asked if I was ready to go to drug treatment. "Yes, ma'am, I sure am."

The social worker told me she had made arrangements for me to go to Olivia's House. I'd never heard of it, but I was willing to go anywhere if I could be with Brittany. She told me the Department of Human Resources (DHR) would require certain things of me during treatment and that keeping Brittany depended on how well I cooperated. I determined right then that I would do everything they asked me to do.

The nurses gave me two baby blankets, two six-packs of baby formula in bottles, and some extra individually wrapped nipples. Brittany had on her hospital gown, and we had that pink teddy bear and the diaper bag that Kathy Campbell had given us. That was the extent of my worldly possessions. I loaded those few things in the social worker's car, and I was the happiest person alive. I didn't even know where we were going.

I felt like a normal woman leaving the hospital with her baby. Christ had given me a new life and I was so content. I was thanking God for this opportunity, whatever it was.

I wasn't thinking about myself as that dirty, lowdown prostitute, crack whore, panhandler, dumpster diver, liar, deceiver, abuser, and accuser. My little girl was in a car seat in the back, and we were on our way to a new life. I was nervous and concerned about what would be expected of me, but I had no doubt about it being the right thing to do.

We drove a long way and turned down a gravel road and through a wide open gate. This was Daniel Payne Drive, and I was going to Olivia's House, a residential treatment center.

When we drove past the cafeteria on the right, I could see big tables and chairs and something that looked like a serving line. Women and children were sitting at tables eating lunch. We came to a two-story building with window air conditioners jutting out from each room. Flower beds lined the entrance. This would be my home for the next 14 months.

When I arrived at Olivia's House, I had only the few articles I mentioned. I didn't have a toothbrush, toothpaste, hairbrush, shampoo, or any other kind of personal hygiene products. I didn't even have any official identification, like a driver's license or Social Security card.

But I knew I had God and He was helping me. I was beginning a new life. Was I scared? Was I afraid of change? In some ways, yes, but I was so excited that I was going to a safe place and that I had my baby with me. Nothing else mattered.

I got checked in and taken to my room. There was a twin bed and a rocking chair. No sheets, towels, blankets, or anything else. When I sat down on the bed, the slat gave way and one corner of the bed collapsed. I fixed that and sat down in the rocking chair. The side rail on the chair came loose and clattered to the floor. I sat in the floor, holding my baby, and began to cry. Loneliness swept over me.

Lord, how can I do this? I don't even have sheets for my bed. I don't have anything to start with, and I don't know anything about taking care of a baby. About that time, there was a knock on the door and a girl who was a resident of Olivia's House came in with a towel and washcloth. She said she had some extra and could give these to me. Somebody found some sheets and a blanket and brought them to me. There was a clothes closet where people gave donations, and they told me I could go through it the next day and find some clothes.

God was already taking care of me in my new home. I knew we were going to be OK. There were many adjustments, but this was the first time I had ever gone into rehab and I wanted it to be the only time. I was determined to do everything I could — with God's help — to start a new life, a life without addiction.

I quickly fell into the daily routine. We all had assigned chores, so I would get up early, eat my breakfast, feed Brittany, do my chores, and be ready for class by 8:30 every morning. In the evening, I'd have my homework to do. I'd journal, read my Bible or other Christian literature, and take care of Brittany. My life was full of joy. I'd look in the mirror and sometimes not even be able to realize how much life had changed.

I was serious about everything that was offered at Olivia's House. I attended all my classes and opened my heart and mind to everything God had to teach me. I loved every minute of it. My counselor helped me delve into why I had chosen the life I did and all the secrets I'd buried deep within me for so many years. I wanted to get to the bottom of this canyon I had created, to know why I acted the way I did.

Being at Olivia's House was my opportunity to get some answers. I talked about my mom and dad and how I blamed them for so much. I talked about my husbands and all the men in my life and how they had used and abused me. My counselor helped me to see that I had to take responsibility and face up to what I had done and the choices I had made.

Every class was important to me and every treatment plan was full of vital information to help me understand myself and my life. I wanted to do everything to make sure I didn't go back to my old ways. God had brought me out of the muck and mire and dirt, and I wanted this new life more than anything. And I sure didn't want to lose this precious little girl He gave me. I was determined to give it my best shot.

Some of the girls would come to class and just clam up and not say anything, but not me. I knew I had to examine it and talk about it. I had lived in such a dark world, but now I wanted everything out in the light. I didn't want to hide anything or forget anything. Somehow I knew that for me to be completely healed, I had to dig out all the hidden corners and confess them and give it all to God. I did just that in those next few months. I figured the more I dealt with, the cleaner I'd become.

Brittany was growing like a weed, and every doctor's visit confirmed that she was a sweet, normal, healthy little girl. I was so thankful and blessed.

A lot of the girls at Olivia's House couldn't wait to get out, but I was glad to be there and to be learning everything. Some classes were required, but we also had some choices about meetings and classes. I went to every one. I couldn't get enough. I was not only learning how to live; through the parenting class I was also learning how to be a mother.

I signed up for the UAB Early Head Start Program. It was strictly voluntary, but I wanted to learn how to be the best mother I could possibly be. I didn't know anything about child development or what to expect. Didn't know when to expect her to roll over or sit up or anything like that. So the Head Start worker, Annie Hunter, would assess her cognitive skills and make sure she was doing everything appropriate for her age level. She'd check things like movements, eye coordination, and motor skills.

Annie and I would meet privately in my room and she'd look at Brittany and test her for all these developmental things, and we'd talk and laugh and get to know each other. She helped me know what things to look for in Brittany's growth and development.

Every Monday night, a church group would come and teach the Bible. We'd discuss different Scriptures, sing a couple of praise songs, and pray together. This was not required, but I went every week.

I also had a radio in my room and I listened to the Christian radio stations. I loved the gospel music and sermons by Adrian Rogers, Charles Stanley, David Jeremiah, and many others. I was so hungry to learn God's Word. I couldn't get enough. I started writing some of those radio pastors and sending a dollar or two when I could. They sent me loads of books and materials. I loved reading all this great information. The other girls would tease me about how much mail I got. I looked forward to all of it.

I was now getting food stamps and a monthly welfare check for $135. Of course, Olivia's House got the food stamps to help provide our food, and I was very careful how I spent the welfare check. I would buy Brittany's diapers and other necessities like shampoo and deodorant and things like that. I was still smoking and I would buy a couple of packs of cigarettes and would only smoke two or three a day to make them last longer.

This was the first time in years that I'd had wholesome meals, except for the times I was at my mother's house. Some of the girls complained about the food, but I thought it was the best I'd ever eaten. The workers in the cafeteria became my good friends. They cared about me and my baby. They even prayed with me and with some of the other girls.

One of the maintenance workers was a godly man, and he started teaching us a Bible study. There were usually not more than four women there, but we studied and learned together. Those were wonderful evenings for me.

I loved the structure and accountability of Olivia's House. At 41, was it difficult for me to take instructions and authority from another adult? Did it make me feel like I was a little teenager at home with a mother over me? Not at all. God had changed me to make that possible, because in the past I never wanted anybody telling me what to do even if they did it in a nice way. Now I knew just how much I needed other people's wisdom and how much I could learn from them.

When I went to Olivia's House, Tom was in jail, but I knew he would find me when he got out. Olivia's House has a rule that if a family member planned on visiting on a Saturday, they had to attend a class on the previous Thursday night.

I didn't know if Tom would be willing to participate, but he did come. I got to see him from across the room. My feelings for him instantly fired up, and I wanted to hold him and feel his arms around me. I wanted to show Brittany to him.

During our supervised visits in the next few weeks, he told me a lot of stuff about how he was working on a new job and things were going so well for him. He'd tell me things he knew I wanted to hear, but I soon realized it was just a game. He said he was off drugs and was doing well. He didn't want to lose me, but I felt in my heart that he wasn't being honest.

After I'd been at Olivia's House about a month, I called my mother and told her where I was and that she had a little grand-daughter. My mother had gone through so much with me by now that I don't think she knew what to think about this. I believe she was totally numb from all my ups and downs. She let me know that she wouldn't be coming out to visit me or making any commitments for when I got out. I understood that, but, of course, it hurt a little too.

But in my spirit, I heard God's Spirit saying, *In time, all in My time, Janet. Right now, it's about you and Me and that little baby girl. It's about making the most of the treatment center opportunities. It's about delving deep into yourself and finding out who you are. It's about reading and studying My Word and finding meaning in me. It's about seeking Me, Janet.*

And I knew that was exactly the right answer. My focus needed to be extremely narrow. I needed to take care of Brittany and myself and I needed to grow in wisdom with the Lord. That's all. I didn't need complications in my life right now. *In time. In time.*

Brittany and I had arrived at Olivia's House on November 14, 2000, the fourth day after she was born, so that first Christmas was really special for us. I got there too late to sign up for any of the lists for people to adopt children or families and provide Christmas gifts, but I didn't worry about that. From the time we came in, the women there had given us part of what they had, and we had benefited from other donations also.

During that first month at Olivia's House, I'd gotten some clothes from the clothes closet for Brittany and for me. Third Presbyterian Church — Ted Pearson's church — had given me some baby items, a Bible, and a radio so I could listen to the preachers I enjoyed so much.

We were getting so many things provided for us that it really didn't matter that we weren't on anybody's Christmas list. At that time, I hadn't been there long enough for a pass, so we spent Christmas at Olivia's House. There was a Christmas tree in the lobby. I was able to take a phone call from my mother, and we said "I love you" to each other. I was given a bag with some baby clothes and a sweater for me. Those were our Christmas gifts.

This was the first Christmas in years that I'd been sober since I was a young teenager and certainly the first one that I knew anything about the true meaning of Christmas. So what better Christmas could there be? I'm still having wonderful Christmases. Actually, now, 12 years later, Brittany and I help get donations together to take to the women at Olivia's House, and that's always a big part of our Christmas. What a blessing that is!

On that first Christmas at Olivia's House, I had the gift of God, a whole new life, and my beautiful baby girl. That's all I needed.

Chapter 19

MY DECISION FOR PURITY

After a few weeks, I was eligible for a weekend pass. Tom and I had made arrangements to be together. He was living in a motel room on Valley Avenue. It was nice enough. Two full-size beds, cable TV, and a little kitchenette area. Tom sent a cab to get me and Brittany. I was excited to see him, but I was also nervous.

At least for the weekend, we're going to be a happy little family. Of course, at that time, there was no way I knew who Brittany's father was. Without drugs and alcohol, I knew Tom could be a good daddy, and I let myself think about what our future might be together. I allowed myself to see us in a fantasy like the families on the TV commercials. With this job, Tom could be a good provider for our family and I'd be a good wife and mother. No more abuse, cursing, doping, or drinking. We would go to church together and raise this precious little girl.

That night we slept together for the first time in a long time. Afterward, I felt dirty and shamed. I had a deep-down feeling that it was very wrong. Honestly, I felt like a prostitute all over again. Ugly and nasty.

The next day, I invited Mother to come and meet her granddaughter. I saw my mother smile for the first time in many years. I think Mother was afraid to look into the future because she had done that with me on many occasions and it had never worked out before.

Tom went to work for a little while that day and Mother stayed and helped me do laundry downstairs in the community laundry room. Mom was an expert on everything about keeping house.

She had the most perfect house. Everything clean and organized and in its place.

When Mom got ready to leave, I told her I loved her. She slipped me $10 and said, "Janet, I love you too."

We really didn't know how to be a mother and daughter. Over the years, so many things had crowded out a normal relationship. But I was determined we could learn. We had never been able to open our hearts to each other. But now we both began to work on learning to love and to communicate, and to develop over time such a sweet mother-daughter relationship.

Mother eventually came to know the Lord, and we talked about Him and prayed together. We still disagreed from time to time, but we loved each other without getting angry and screaming and cursing to show our feelings. I loved her just as she was, and she loved me just as I was.

Later that second day with Tom, when he came back from work, I didn't know how to express to him about all that the Lord was convicting me about in my heart. But together we were able to enjoy watching Brittany.

On Sunday morning, I got a ride to Third Presbyterian Church with a friend. It was so good to get to worship in a real church and be with Christians. It truly felt like home to me. That afternoon, I returned to Olivia's House. In a way, it was hard to leave Tom, but I was ready to get back to my new routine, to the place that had become so comfortable for me.

When I was checking back in, they examined my packages and did a urine test for drugs. Everything was fine, of course.

I went to my room to get ready for my Monday classes, and the Lord was convicting me so strongly. I heard His Spirit telling me, *Janet, I want all of you. I saved you and called you by name that day on that table. I want all of you to belong to Me.*

How in the world could I worship, praise, and thank God for all He had done, but yet hold on to this part of my life that wanted to lie down and be with a man who wasn't my husband?

In bed that night, I sobbed my heart out because I knew I had disappointed the Lord. But from that moment, I knew I could never be intimate with another man who wasn't my husband. I realized that if God chose to give me a husband, whether it was Tom or someone else, it would be a wonderful moment when I gave myself to him. If not, I knew I would remain pure.

Pure! How could I even use that word? The Lord didn't take away my past. That ugly past was still there in full detail, but He did take away the condemnation. "Therefore, there is now no condemnation for those who are in Christ Jesus, because through Christ Jesus the law of the Spirit of life set me free from the law of sin and death" (Romans 8:1). But He expected me to do what he asked of me, and that is to remain pure from that day forward. God radically changed my life, including my thinking and understanding about sin and my attitude about what is acceptable before Him.

A couple of weeks later, I had another weekend pass. I was excited to see Tom again, but I was really anxious. *How would he react to my decision?*

Tom sent a cab to get me. On the way to the motel where we were going to stay, I was thinking about how I could tell him. I was asking the Lord to help me. I believed that we would get married and live happily together with Brittany. It was just a matter of time. Each of us had things to work on, but I thought marriage was surely in our future.

Tom was really antsy that weekend. He was different from the last pass. He would offer to go get me something, maybe a soda or some chips. I'd say no, but he would disappear anyway, come back for a few minutes, and then say, "Oh, I forgot to get my chips. I'll be right back," but he'd be gone 20 minutes or more.

This happened several times, but I was so happy with all three of us being together that I didn't catch on at first. I didn't even try to figure it out. I was still worrying about what would happen when we went to bed and he wanted me.

Well, he came back from supposedly doing laundry downstairs and I looked him in the face and said, "Tom, you're high! You've smoked crack! Why are you doing this?"

I could see it in his face and eyes. I was in shock. Of course, he said, "No, oh no, you're crazy. I'm not doing anything."

I said, "Tom, I got high with you for seven years and I know how you act and how I act. I can tell. Why are you doing this? Why are you doing this to me now? Why are you doing this in front of your daughter?"

"Well, I'm trying to get clean. This is only a $20 rock and then there won't be any more. Just a couple of hits left." I was holding Brittany in my arms while we were talking. I was completely devastated. I guess I should have known it wouldn't be easy, but I had so hoped and prayed it would. I thought all that was over and behind both of us.

That weekend showed me that the man I thought would be my husband didn't truly love me. Not enough to stay clean. He wanted the old Janet back, the one he could beat on and control and have sex with whenever he wanted.

When we were getting ready for bed, I knew what Tom wanted, but I told him I couldn't do it. I told him how nasty it made me feel and that I didn't want to feel that way anymore. He picked up the phone, the nearest thing to him, and was going to hit me with it or maybe choke me with the cord, but I calmly stood there with my little girl in my arms. "I'm not afraid of you anymore. You'll never hit me or hurt me again. I'm not the crack whore you used to know."

I prayed, *God, protect me and keep me safe. Please, God, I can't lose what I have.* And God answered. He covered me with His love and protection that night and taught me a valuable lesson too. I would never go on a weekend pass to a motel with Tom again.

I learned another thing that weekend. I had spent years giving myself to men and doing horrible, vulgar things. But that was over. Now I saw my body as the temple of God, and He was living in me. I had defiled that temple by being with Tom.

I slept in one bed that night and Tom slept in the other. The next day, Sunday, I went to church and Tom went to work. That afternoon I returned to Olivia's House and tested clean. I managed to make it through those temptations only because God had strengthened me. I felt stronger inside than I ever had, and I knew God was going to protect me from times like that weekend and from other temptations in the future.

My mother started letting me come to her house on my passes every other weekend. She would always cook good food and enjoy being with Brittany. I would work on my homework assignments while I was there. I didn't feel like I had to prove anything to my mother any more. She saw what was happening in me. God broke down the Great Wall of China that had been between us for so many years.

Those weekends were so peaceful and calm and loving. Mom and I learned how to listen to each other. God truly mends relationships that people have destroyed. He made that happen between me and my mother. This time spent together was a healing time for our relationship.

God helped me see things about my parents and to stop blaming them for some of my own mistakes. I never thought my mother loved me, but now I know she did the best she could at the time.

There are times when I'm tired or busy and I'd rather not stop what I'm doing and answer Brittany or listen to her tell me something for the millionth time. But I know how important it is for her to know that I am listening and that I do care. I don't want her to grow up with the feeling of not being loved. I want to shower her with love and time and attention. That doesn't mean material things, but just being available to her. I want more than anything to teach her the ways of God.

I don't want my daughter to reach out to someone for love at an early age because she hasn't received love at home. I'm doing all I can to love her and to have people around her who love her and show her what a life dedicated to God really means.

Some of us from difficult childhoods reached for the bottle or the drug or the sick relationship. We've hung out with the wrong kinds of friends and gotten involved in wrong activities. I think all the way back to when I was 13 and met Don and how I was looking for love. I craved attention and when he held me and kissed me and made me feel loved, I thought I had found that love. But look where that got me. I am doing my best to teach Brittany to make wiser decisions.

Brittany and I talk openly about whatever is appropriate for her age. We've always done that. I realize that teenagers and young adults are not always willing to receive wisdom from their parents, but talking with Brittany is not all I'm doing. Every day I pray that God will protect her from evil and guide me in raising her. When it all is said and done, Brittany is His girl, and He's given me the miracle of being her mother.

Chapter 20

ONE MORE BIG STEP —NEW TEETH!

After Christmas, the people at Third Presbyterian Church said they wanted to do something special for me. They asked me what I needed. I didn't know what to ask for. They had done so much and, really, all our needs were being met. But they told me to pray about it, so I did.

Their offer made me start thinking about life after Olivia's House. I knew I wouldn't be in recovery forever, and I didn't want to live on a welfare check for any longer than I had to. I wanted someday to be able to have a job again and for Brittany and me to have our own place to live. I had accepted that I would never be able to work at a hospital again because I had lost my x-ray tech license. I hadn't kept up continuing education units and, if I reapplied, I was sure my criminal record and numerous times in jail would be held against me.

But I knew I wanted to work and eventually be independent. One of the things that would help me be ready for a job was to have some dental work done. My teeth were rotten, chipped, and broken as a result of the drug use and from being hit in the mouth so many times.

So Third Presbyterian arranged for me to see Dr. William Buck, an oral surgeon in Birmingham. Ted Pearson made the appointment for me and provided transportation to appointments. Dr. Buck did x-rays and other examinations and determined that most of my teeth would need to come out. For some that were broken into the gum line, that meant taking them out by the roots. I had only four teeth that were worth saving.

In treatment, no pain medication is allowed, so I understood that I would not be able to use prescription pain relievers. I would have been expelled from Olivia's House for using those kinds of medications.

Dr. Buck explained that he was going to have to open my gums to remove the teeth and stitch all the way across each gum. He told me I would be bruised and that it would be difficult to eat anything except mushy food for a while. After my gums healed, I would get dentures. The whole process would take about three months.

I had explained to Dr. Buck that I couldn't take prescription pain medication, and he understood. He told me they would put a mask on and give me a little "gas" so that I would be relaxed. As soon as I started feeling the effects of the gas, I thought, *Oh no, I'm getting high. I can't do this.* I just couldn't take any chances of feeling high and liking it again.

So Dr. Buck gave me shots with long needles in my gums. He warned me that it would be rough and it was. This procedure took a long time, and my mouth and lips were really numb the rest of the day. The next day, I looked like I had crashed into an 18-wheeler. My face was black and my eyes were swollen. My mouth ached terribly. It's a good thing I didn't have any pain medication around except acceptable over-the-counter pain medicine because I probably would have been tempted to take it.

I wasn't able to eat much for several weeks. I drank liquids and pureed food through a straw. When the stitches were finally taken out, Ted took me to Oxford, Alabama, where Dr. Rick Mitchell fitted me with dentures. They looked beautiful. I'm so grateful to Third Presbyterian Church, Ted, Dr. Buck, and Dr. Mitchell for helping me. What huge blessings they were!

I guess by this time in my recovery I was beginning to see things in a little bit lighter and more humorous way, so I played a trick on my friends at Olivia's House. Trying to be helpful, my mother had given me a pair of dentures that she had years ago.

They were huge! I cleaned them and put them in my mouth. All you could see was this huge mouthful of teeth. I looked horrible!

So on the day I was scheduled to receive my new dentures, I strolled back into Olivia's House, smiling really big with those hideous dentures, and all the women looked kind of shocked when they first saw me. Not wanting to hurt my feelings, they would say, "Oh, oh, well, they look really, uh, pretty, Janet." No doubt they were all extremely relieved when they saw my real new teeth and realized I'd been playing a joke on them.

Becoming a jokester, I guess, was just a result of the happiness inside me. Being clean and sober and living in a nice place, learning about myself and learning more about God, all of that just made me a happy, satisfied, and contented person. I still like to play pranks!

In one of our donation bags, there were some tennis shoes that had taps on the bottom. Olivia's House had tile floors and I would put on those tap shoes and dance all around Brittany's stroller. Sometimes I'd come into class and start tap dancing. Everyone would laugh, and we'd have a good time with it. I kept those shoes for years and then put them in another donation bag to give to someone else.

With all the jokes and the fun times, we also had some sad times at Olivia's House. Everyone there, of course, had come with bruises and scars. But we also laughed a lot.

I mostly remember the laughter.

Chapter 21

GROWING AND LEARNING

I could hardly believe how many ways the Lord was changing me while I was at Olivia's House. I enjoyed going to bed at 8:30 or 9:00 in the evening and just being in the room with my baby girl. Me, the woman who never slept and who caroused around all night only living for the next crack high.

Even things like doing laundry was such a joy for me. Washing my clothes and Brittany's and folding them neatly and placing them in our dresser and closet—I loved it! Again, this is the woman who wore the same outfit for weeks at a time and dug a new one out of a dumpster or garbage bag.

Having our own bathroom, my own towel and washcloth, a shower every day, clean sheets on my bed—even having a bed!—this was heaven to me. And that I got to share it with my child was even better.

I enjoyed three good meals a day. Even to this day, 12 years later, sometimes I feel like I can't get full. All those years of being hungry gave me a great appreciation for food.

Sure, there were things I didn't have. I didn't have much free time. I was always in class or doing chores except for a brief time at night. I didn't have freedom to come and go as I pleased. I didn't have a car. I continually had people telling me what to do and where to be.

I didn't let any of that bind me up. No, ma'am. I was totally happy to comply with all the rules and expectations at Olivia's House. I was getting another start. I was safe and warm and my stomach was full. My child was sleeping beside me every night.

Our future looked bright. It's true that I didn't have many material possessions. What I did have couldn't be measured in dollars and cents.

I could have been in prison or dead. I could have been out there on the streets wondering where I could get $5. I was so overwhelmingly grateful to be where I was.

Please don't get the idea that I instantly shucked off all my bad habits and became Miss Perfect. Not so. I was still smoking, as I said. I didn't really even want to address that yet. Now and then I'd utter a curse word. Sometimes anger or rudeness would flare up inside me.

We're all human and we all fall short. It's easy to say that anger or gossip isn't a sin that compares with smoking dope or selling my body, but God's Word tells me He hates all sin. Sin is sin. I cry out to the Lord and say, *Lord God, help me! I don't want to feel this way or act this way.* He has dealt with me on so many things and He continues to work on me. I'll never forget where I was and what I did and how much He's changed me.

Even after all these years of walking with God, I can cry so quickly when I think of all He's done for me. *Lord, how I love You. How I love the life You've given me.* And now I can even be thankful for the old life because I really, truly appreciate that He actually died to save me. Deliverance has helped me know Who the Deliverer is. And today I believe in Janet too. He put a new strength in me with a mind, abilities, and talents to work for Him. It's all because of Him.

Being at Olivia's House was a wonderful time for me and for Brittany, too, because I was learning to be her mother. My UAB Early Head Start caseworker, Annie Hunter, came often to see Brittany. She was doing everything exactly as she was supposed to for her age. Lifting her head, rolling over, moving her arms, trying to crawl, following objects with her eyes. She wasn't behind on a thing! How wonderful and precious is that? Brittany didn't suffer any physical problems because of my sin and abuse. If I didn't have anything else to praise God for, that would be enough!

I was making some really good friends at Olivia's House among the staff—my counselor, Yvas Witherspoon, my teachers, Gail and Karen, and some of the maintenance staff. I enjoyed the ladies who came to lead Bible study on Monday nights and the occasional worship service.

My caseworker from the Department of Human Resources (welfare) was Sabrina Bristow. And how about this for a God-ordained "coincidence"? Sabrina had been my caseworker just a couple of years before when Brandon was born. At that time, I blamed her and hated her because my son was taken away from me. Now God was showing me that the problem was not a DHR worker; I was the problem.

Of course, I don't want to give the impression that everything in recovery or in Olivia's House was mushy sweet and fun. We had some difficult times too. Sometimes girls would even fistfight. They'd get angry about something and end up tumbling around in the floor, pounding each other.

There were a lot of rules at Olivia's House. We couldn't be in each other's rooms. We had to be in our own rooms at 8:30 with lights out by 9:00 nightly. We had to attend classes and do chores. Of course, those with children had some extra rules about the children.

Sometimes women who left on a pass would bring back drugs. Even though they were always caught and expelled, I wanted to stay as far away from that as possible because I sure didn't want to have to leave. There were even a few off-limits relationships in the house. When the counselors found out, those women were also expelled.

In the spring, my counselor approached me about starting a job readiness program and applying for a housing voucher. If accepted, I would attend some classes, get a job, and then be able to move into approved housing somewhere around Birmingham. I knew I wasn't ready for this. I asked God to show me if I just wasn't ready to leave the security of my situation or if it really wasn't my time to leave. I felt sure God was leading me to stay a little longer, so I continued my classes and working on treatment plans, studying my Bible and other Christian literature, and taking care of Brittany.

One of the other residents, Tina, told me her sister had a car for sale. It was a two-door , very faded silver color like it had been painted with primer. It was a five-speed car with bucket seats. Tina's sister was from the North, so this car had been driven in snow and ice and had lots of rust underneath. But I thought it was beautiful.

The asking price was $750. I didn't have that much, although I had been able to save $250 from my $135-a-month welfare checks. Ted Pearson offered to lend me $250 and we made a deal to buy the car for $500. A wonderful friend, Cherry, who was a former resident at Olivia's House, gave me a set of used tires for the car. I was ecstatic!

Of course, I had to get permission to buy it, and I couldn't drive it except when given approval. I paid Ted Pearson $25 a month for ten months until I had repaid the loan. That Ted would still have enough faith in me to help was amazing since I had taken advantage of him so many times in the past. His unfaltering friendship through the years has been a precious gift to me.

Soon after going to Olivia's House I started a journal and I wrote my heart out every chance I got. It seemed like every time I sat down with pen and paper I had so much to say. Pages and pages of memories kept tumbling out of me. Putting my life on paper was one way I had of taking responsibility for my past. And each day and each week, God was healing me and helping me understand myself.

All God wanted me to do was keep going to my classes, keep listening, keep giving it my best, and doing whatever it took to leave my old life behind. I needed to expose whatever trash I had put inside myself for all those years, and all this took time. I just thank Him that He was giving me that ability more and more each day.

I continued to take my weekend passes and go to Mom's. When we went to bed at night, we'd both say "I love you" and in the morning, she'd cook me a big breakfast. Sometimes we'd talk about my future and what I hoped for, but I really didn't try to get too far ahead. I was still totally astounded by the life I was living from day to day.

Sometimes when I was on a pass to visit Mom, I would attend an AA meeting in Trussville, near Birmingham, where she lived. Actually, that became my "home group." They were a wonderful group of encouraging people, and, although I went to AA meetings at Olivia's House and other places, too, that Trussville group was very special to me.

I remember one time telling Mom about how it helped me and how I really admired some of the people in the group, and she said, "I wish so much your father had been able to have that." Well, I do too. If only he had, maybe his life would have been totally different.

Many people live with a lot of "if onlys." Now and then, I let myself look back on three decades of a life full of sin and poor decisions. *If only I hadn't become sexually active so young. If only I hadn't taken that first puff of a marijuana cigarette. If only I had grown up in the church and heard about God's ways sooner. If only I'd believed.*

But I don't allow my mind to go there often. Those if onlys were erased that day on the delivery table when God spoke so clearly to my spirit and invited me to follow Him.

PATHWAYS AND CHRISTIAN WOMEN'S JOB CORPS

About four months after I'd decided against the job readiness program, my counselor, Yvas, approached me again. This time I knew I was ready, so we began putting the pieces together so I could attend the classes. While I was gone, Brittany stayed in day care at Olivia's House. I was given permission to drive my little junker car to class in downtown Birmingham.

The name of the program was Birmingham Path (now called Pathways), a nonprofit organization funded by United Way and various other entities, as well as individual donations. It was another wonderful new experience for me. As part of the training, every day a special speaker would come in to talk with us about a different topic. Sometimes they'd talk about job opportunities and how to prepare for a job interview. One lady talked about commitment and taking responsibility. Someone else came and talked to us about budgeting and getting out of debt.

One speaker talked about self-esteem and confidence, and one time we even had a lady who was a beauty products consultant come in and teach us about makeup. That was a really fun time. We sat around and laughed and talked. She told us we were all pretty on the inside and she would help us improve our appearance on the outside.

I felt great pride in going to class and keeping my notebook neat and organized. It's hard to put into words what was happening to me, but life was definitely taking on a whole new meaning. I had hope that someday I could again be a productive person, going to work every day and making my own living.

Barbara White from the Human Resources Department at UAB Hospital came to speak to us one day. She talked about job opportunities there and how important it is to be confident during an interview and to present yourself honestly and straightforwardly. She said UAB was expanding in several departments and there might be job possibilities for some of us if we were interested.

Barbara took a special interest in each person that day and expressed such kindness and encouragement to all of us, like she believed in us even though she didn't know us. I told her I had worked for UAB in the early 1980s and had been an x-ray tech in the Birmingham area for 11 years. I admitted that I had lost my license, so I knew it wouldn't be possible for me to work in x-ray. But I told her I would love to talk with her about the possibility of working in dietary or housekeeping. I knew UAB was one of the best employers in Birmingham. My goal was to get a job that provided health insurance and retirement and not have to rely on food stamps or Medicaid.

She encouraged me to come and talk with her when I finished Pathways. I held onto that prospect and determined to work harder to complete the program and learn all I could. I was excited to think that working again at UAB was a possibility.

The bond that developed among the women at Pathways was unique. We laughed together and cried a few times, too, when we discussed our past mistakes. But we all had such high hopes for something better for the future. Our teacher, Cathy, loved us and we grew to love each other. I had never been part of a group like this before where I related to other women in an encouraging and uplifting way. We were all taking steps forward in our lives and I loved every minute of it.

Graduation from Pathways was on the horizon and I was excited. I had never really graduated from anything. I didn't finish high school but, instead, took the GED exam. When I had finished x-ray training at Jefferson State Community College, I didn't go through the graduation ceremony. I didn't care and, really, no one else in my life at that time cared, either.

Pathways graduation was held at a church near the training facility and we were allowed to invite anyone we wanted. My cheering section that day included my mother, my pastor's wife from Third Presbyterian, Mary Eleanor Trucks, and her friend Susan Simon, Yvas Witherspoon, Annie Hunter, Kathy Campbell, and Ted and Karen Pearson.

The graduates lined up at the back of the church and they played the same music for the processional that you hear at high school or college graduations. As I walked down that aisle, I was grinning ear-to-ear and crying huge tears of joy. It was the best day and the best feeling I'd had in a long time.

I have two photographs from that day, one of all these people who had been so important in my life and one of me and all the other graduates. I cherish those pictures. Graduation from Pathways was the first big milestone in my new life.

Another person I met at Pathways was Anita Neur, who was director of the Christian Women's Job Corps® (CWJC®), a ministry of Woman's Missionary Union® (WMU®), Auxiliary to Southern Baptist Convention. She came and spoke to us before graduation and invited us to be a part of CWJC. She explained that they would have classes similar to the ones we'd had at Pathways and they would also pair each woman with a mentor.

Our mentors would be Christian women, probably older than us. We could meet for Bible study or just have some discussions about what was going on in our lives. Anita explained that this mentor would not be a person who would supply us with money, be a babysitter, or be someone we could take advantage of in any way. This would be a woman who wanted to be a guide and to share the love of God.

I made application to CWJC and was accepted, as were several other women from my Pathways class. I was scared and excited at the same time. I knew nothing about having a mentor and I wasn't sure how I felt about it, but it sounded like a great idea to have a mature Christian woman to talk with.

So the afternoon of our first meeting, when we would be matched with our mentors, I put Brittany in her little car seat and drove to the meeting. As I was getting Brittany out of the car, another lady drove up. Anita was standing outside and she brought this lady over to me and introduced us. I had no idea she would end up being my mentor—and I sure had no idea how important she would be in my life from that day forward—but her gentleness and sweetness made me feel instantly at ease.

Was I hungry for this kind of guidance from a mature Christian woman who wanted to be my mentor? You bet I was. I was excited about this whole new life and I was hungry for everything I could get. I'm not talking about material things. I'm talking about experiences and relationships. I'm talking about acceptance and love and compassion. I wanted to know how to do the right things and learn how to make right choices. I wanted help in thinking things through as a child of God so I wouldn't make the same bad decisions I had made in the past.

God gave me a miracle when he put June Whitlow in my life as my mentor and my friend. I prayed every morning for God to guide my day and help me be obedient to Him, and the day I met June Whitlow was a day He had planned for both of us.

June and I can laugh today about what was going on in each of our minds at that first meeting. I wondered if June would be afraid I'd steal her wallet or take advantage of her in some way. She says she had never even met anyone with a background like mine, so she wondered if she would be able to relate to me. June is a seminary graduate, the daughter of a Southern Baptist preacher, and she's worked all her life in a Christian vocation. So it's true that on that day we were two women from totally different experiences, but we came together because God planned it that way.

We signed a covenant for a three-month relationship through CWJC. During the next few weeks, we studied the Bible together and talked by phone. Sometimes we met and talked. June came several times to visit us at Olivia's House. When our three-month agreement was completed, we personally decided to sign another covenant, then another, and another. After that, we didn't see any need to sign covenants. By then we were part of each other's lives, and that's the way it still is today.

When I met June, I thought she was all the things I was not. She was beautiful and perfect. So clean! She was gracious and polite and shining. When I say she was shining, I mean that there was something about her that made me know instantly that she was real. She was not a goody-goody wanting to help a poor girl. Actually, she did want to help me, but she was just letting Jesus' love shine through her.

I'd never known anyone like June. In the past, when I met people like June, I wouldn't want to be with them. I'd never cared about knowing good people — or God's people. I just wanted to be with the party crowd and the dope crowd.

I wondered if June would see me and think of me as a lowdown, filthy, imperfect sinner. She never, ever treated me that way. It's kind of like how we are when we come to Christ. We have to believe that, even with all our sin, He can accept us and love us and change us.

June was — and still is — the image of Christ here on earth to me.

Chapter 23

OUR FIRST HOME

During the first part of December 2001, I made an appointment for an interview with Barbara White in the Human Resources Department at UAB. After we talked, she walked me through the radiology department. I saw several people I remembered from working there years ago. Of course, they recognized me. "Janet, where have you been? What have you been doing?"

I didn't have time right then to tell them the whole story, but I just told them I hoped to be hired and maybe I'd see them soon. Because my license had expired, I really had given up hope of getting a job in radiology, but, as I told Barbara, I would be so happy to get a job in housekeeping and to be able to work for a wonderful employer like UAB.

God in His mercy and compassion, made it possible for me to get a job in a student employee position in the radiology department. I was overjoyed at this opportunity and overwhelmingly grateful to the people at UAB—Barbara White, and J. D. Billingsley, the supervisor of the radiology department—for giving me this opportunity. Still yet, I'm awed by the way God worked out all the particulars to give me such a fantastic job.

Although I worked full-time, I was classified as a student worker making an hourly wage of $8.25. This job provided good health insurance for Brittany and me, and I was contributing to the state retirement plan. No longer would I be on Medicaid or food stamps. I had a real job! Thank You, God!

I called June and told her about the job and she was so happy. She told me she was proud of me. I don't know how long it had been since anyone had told me that. I vowed again to do everything possible to keep her trust. I called Mom and she was so proud of me too.

I was to begin work on December 17. Before I had even started the job, Deisha Rosser from Pathways called to say she knew of an apartment that had become vacant and Pathways could help me if I wanted to look at it. I met her on Cotton Avenue at a small brick building with two apartments upstairs and two downstairs. It was one of Pathways' residential homes.

The apartment Deisha showed me was on the bottom left. It had hardwood floors, built-in bookshelves, and a few pieces of furniture. There was a little kitchen and two small bedrooms. Each apartment had a porch or a balcony. I instantly loved it!

I explained to Deisha that it would be a week before I started my job and then it would be at least two weeks before I got a paycheck. Deisha said that wasn't a problem and handed me a key.

"What?"

"It's yours," she said.

I literally fell to my knees and cried. My first home! My daughter's first home! Not only did I have a wonderful job, but now I had a real place to live.

Deisha explained the rules. No male visitors. No one could spend the night unless approved. There would be inspections, pop-in visits, and a few more things like that. That was all just fine with me. I would have no problems following the rules. Now, for sure, that was a different me than only about 13 months before!

Deisha also gave me a voucher for $100 to buy scrubs and shoes for work. I hadn't even thought about that, but God had. I also knew I'd need to arrange day care for Brittany. Childcare Services, a United Way agency, helped me with the cost of that too. The agreement with Pathways was that I would give them 30 percent out of each paycheck for my rent, utilities, and (I discovered later) savings. (Pathways is funded by United Way, and ever since I became involved with Pathways, I've been a strong supporter of United Way.)

So I began moving, and right before Christmas Brittany and I were in our new home. Before we left Olivia's House, AmSouth Bank had adopted us for Christmas and they gave Brittany several nice gifts. They provided wonderful things for our new home too. A set of dishes, bowls, silverware, and towels. What a great Christmas!

My life was progressing in the most astounding ways — and at breakneck speed. I was almost independent. Almost a responsible member of society again. Those days of going from one hit to another and one man to another were over. I had to pinch myself to believe the blessings that flooded my life every single day.

Even though I was on my own, I knew I needed a recovery group, so every Tuesday night, Ted and Karen Pearson kept Brittany for me so I could go to Grace and Truth Church. Charles Mozley led that group and actually wrote a book about a 12-step Christian recovery program.

I had a job and a nice, safe place to live. I had Brittany and my church family and my mother. I was building an amazing relationship with June. I was enjoying true friendships with some wonderful women too. One of those was June's friend, Pat Ferguson. Their friendship is so close that I can hardly say "June" without saying "June and Pat."

The folks at the food stamp office told me they would provide food stamps through January, and Medicaid coverage would continue until my UAB health insurance became effective. I was OK with all that. I didn't want to keep using all that when I could be self-supporting.

Susan Simon, my friend from Third Presbyterian Church, asked if she could see the apartment. I was happy and proud to show it to her. Then she asked if she could have the key for a day. *Sure, no problem.*

Well, when Brittany and I walked into that apartment after work the next night, Susan, Jan Whitt, and their crew from Third Presbyterian had done their magic. There was a gold-colored chair with an ottoman, a new full-sized bed with sheets, a comforter, matching pillows, and shams. In Brittany's room, there was a new twin bed and a Cracker Jack comforter, sheets, and pillows. The refrigerator was full of food, and the cabinets were packed with canned goods.

In the bathroom, there were towels, a rug, and a new shower curtain. There were lamps on the end tables and a tablecloth on the table. Even salt and pepper shakers! My home had become a beautiful place, thanks to these beautiful people. How God blessed me. These women still love me and I love them. Many people from Third Presbyterian Church helped me through the years, and I'm so grateful for them.

By Christmas, I had been on the job one week. I started each day early. I'd fix my coffee, read my Bible, and pray. I'd take Brittany to day care and listen outside the door until she stopped crying. On the way to work I'd praise God and pray for her safety.

I was so proud of all this. So filled with joy. This was a way of life that I had never experienced. Everything had new meaning for me because I knew the Lord Jesus Christ. I was living in His grace every single day.

On my job, I was gung ho. I'd clock in and couldn't wait to see who I would meet or who I would get to help. I wasn't hesitant about telling God's story, either. Those people I had known wanted to know where I'd been. I told them. I wanted them to know what a miracle God had done in my life. Through the years, I've also told patients about God's amazing work in my life, and many of those patients have become friends who I still have contact with from time to time.

Over the years since I had last worked, x-ray technology had changed drastically. Everything was digital now. I had a lot to learn, but my co-workers were patient and taught me all the new equipment and procedures. I was an eager student, so it wasn't long until they trusted me with more responsibilities. At the end of the workday, I couldn't wait to get on that shuttle bus, get my rooty-toot car from the parking lot, and drive to the day care to pick up my little girl.

My mother visited me now and then, and she always wanted to bring me something. She might have found a good price on detergent and bought one for me, or just some little something.

I called my son, David, and told him where I was living. He was married by that time and had two little children, my grandchildren. One weekend he came and brought his family to visit us. We both knew we had a long way to go to build a relationship, but this was a great start.

Tom and his boss at that time helped me moved into the apartment, and he would show up from time to time. He wanted to come in and eat or he'd ask for a few dollars. Sometimes he'd want to take a shower or wash his clothes. Occasionally I'd come home and he'd be sitting on my porch. I wanted to help him, but I couldn't. When you've been forgiven, it's important to forgive others, but the rules said I couldn't have a male guest. I couldn't have anyone visit without permission. I wasn't about to break those rules.

Tom had not changed his life, and I couldn't risk losing all I had. I told him I wanted to be his friend, and I would occasionally help him out with a few dollars, but that was all I could do. He'd get mad and curse me out and I'd threaten to call the law. My heart ached for Tom. I prayed for him to change and give his life to God.

My life was really full in those days. I was working, caring for Brittany, and being involved in several groups. We went to Third Presbyterian Church on Sundays and with June to Mountain Brook Baptist Church on Wednesday nights. I went to an AA aftercare group led by Charles Mozley at Grace and Truth Church on Tuesday evenings and to another AA aftercare group near my mother's house in Trussville on Saturdays. Mom would keep Brittany while I went to the meeting and we would often spend the night with her.

Annie Hunter from Early Head Start would come by our house regularly and we'd talk about Brittany's learning skills and development.

After I was settled in the apartment, some of the people from Third Presbyterian wanted to give me a housewarming. Susan

Simon is an excellent caterer, and she planned a wonderful meal. They told me to invite everyone I wanted to. I asked my counselor and friends from Olivia's House and Pathways, Brittany's child-care providers, my pastor and Charles Mozley from Grace and Truth, June and Pat, my mother, and friends from Third Presbyterian.

Susan's husband, Dr. Harold Simon, came and helped serve the food that day. Later, he became my mother's doctor and cared for her when she was dying.

People came and went during the party. They got to see our little apartment and all the things that had been given to us. The ladies from Third Presbyterian gave me a Bible with my name on the cover. I still use that Bible. They also framed a piece of paper on which everyone had written their best wishes, like you would on a greeting card. Brittany and I have that hanging on our wall to this day.

The place was packed. People were talking and laughing and eating. Brittany was running around like she was the star! I can't help but laugh now when I think about that party. That was really a different kind of party than any I'd ever participated in. In my past, parties meant drinking, drugs, getting naked, and a lot of other things. Now, here I was with my little girl and precious Christian friends. How great is our God!

Chapter 24

MORE PROGRESS

Martha Schlaudecker was an intern working with Pathways, and she helped me set some new goals. I'd been receiving lots of bills from old accounts that I'd never paid. I wanted to rebuild my credit, which had been ruined because of all the bad checks and unpaid accounts. Martha and I talked about how I would budget my money and how I could realistically repay these old bills.

I went to bed in peace every night. Although I would sometimes be exhausted from my schedule, I never feared getting hurt or having something horrible happen to me as I had for so many years. I rested in God's arms. What did I have to fear? The days on the street, living in sin and fear, were all gone. I was in God's perfect peace and in the shadow of His wings. Life was going by fast, and I couldn't have been happier. At last, I felt like I was living.

I was off all government assistance, and I was learning to manage my money and my time. Cooking supper, doing the laundry, and keeping our apartment neat kept me busy and happy at home. Drinking or using drugs again was never a thought. I couldn't give up this peaceful time for that hell on earth again. That old desire, which was so overpowering—was gone.

One particularly sad thing came along with the happy times, though. My friend, Lynn, died of an overdose. I went to her funeral. She was still young and beautiful, but her addiction had taken her life. Her friend, Robert, still calls me sometimes, and I recently met her sister-in-law. I know Lynn's family prayed fervently for her over the years.

As life moved along, Martha suggested that I inquire about getting back my x-ray license. I thought it would be a long shot considering my arrest record and everything else in my background, but she thought I should set that as one of my goals. I know God planted that seed in her mind because I never would have thought it was possible. I was incredibly happy working in the student position, but, of course, having my license reinstated would mean a significant hike in pay.

June encouraged me to contact the American Registry of Radiological Technologists (ARRT) to see what would be required for me to regain my license. They sent back information and a reinstatement application.

After I submitted my application, ARRT requested information about the criminal charges and jail terms I'd had through the years. They wanted to know what drugs I'd used and what I'd done in recovery. I gathered many records and letters of recommendation, all of which took months. I was eventually notified that my application would be sent to the ethics committee for review. I thought the prospects for reinstatement were bleak.

I determined not to worry or let it get me down. I knew I couldn't stay in this student job indefinitely; I would need to be licensed within one year or lose my job. But I knew God had brought me to this point, and I was not going to question my tomorrows. I continued to rest in Him daily. My days were full, and God was providing. That's all I needed to know for the present.

Eventually, I got a letter from ARRT saying that I would be eligible for reinstatement as a radiological technologist by reexamination. Reexamination? I hadn't taken a test in years. I'd earned my x-ray license in 1980 by sitting for the licensure exam in a classroom with teachers walking up and down the aisles clocking our time. Now the exam was given on a computer with 200-plus questions. How could I do this? I wasn't sure I knew enough or remembered enough.

I was excited about the opportunity. The thought that I might be a registered x-ray tech again was so far beyond anything I'd hoped for. Pathways gave me $150 to pay for the examination fee and bought me some textbooks to study. The test would include questions on CAT scan, MRI, positioning, physics, safety, and so much that I hadn't studied when I was in school more than 20 years before.

I didn't remember everything I'd learned years ago, but I did remember my dependency on God. *There's no way I can pass this test without You, God.* I set out to study, but, of course, life was going on. Working and taking care of Brittany, plus everything else I had to do made it really difficult to study.

June was praying for me through this, and our relationship had grown so close by this time that I really depended on her encouragement and advice. A few days after I took the exam, June, Brittany, and I were scheduled to go to St. Louis for a national meeting of WMU—again, the organization that sponsors Christian Women's Job Corps (CWJC). We had been asked to tell the women there about our experience of being a mentor and mentee with CWJC and beyond.

As we were on the way to the airport to board the plane to St. Louis, my mother called and said I had received a letter from ARRT. I'd heard that a big envelope meant you passed and a small envelope meant you failed.

"How big is the envelope?" I asked my mother.

"Just a regular envelope," she said. I told her to open it and read it to me.

"Oh Janet," she said. "You didn't make it." The passing score was 75 and I had made a 73. I burst into tears. I was on my way to catch a plane and speak to a huge crowd of ladies about what God had done for me and now I'd failed. I felt overwhelming defeat.

But I did realize how much God had changed me, because I didn't immediately think, like in the old days, *I've got to have a drink* or *I've got to have a hit.* Now I only thought about how sad I was and how I had wanted this so much. I didn't want to disappoint the people who had supported me while I prepared for the exam.

"You can take the test again," June said. "You'll just study harder and you can do it."

We had a fabulous time in St. Louis. June and I told our story to about 400 women. I remember how honored I felt. June's sister, Nancy—Aunt Nancy to us now—sat in the audience with Brittany. June had bought me a nice dress, and I was proud of the way I looked. I still have that dress.

Before we started speaking, I went to the bathroom and prayed that God would speak through me. I knew God would have His will through me that day. That was in 2003 and I've been asked to speak and tell my story—God's story—hundreds of times since then. I never write anything down or plan what I'm going to say. I depend completely on God to speak through me, and He never fails.

I love telling His story, how He came to me on the delivery table that day and how He continues to care for me and Brittany. Every time I tell it, I become stronger and more aware of how real His presence is in my life. We all have stories of what God has done for us, and I want to continue to tell what He's done for me as long as He gives me breath to do it.

The trip to St. Louis encouraged me so much. Standing in front of all those women was something I could never have imagined I'd be able to do. Testifying about what God did for me and how He used CWJC to bless me and how much it meant to have June Whitlow as my mentor was an experience I'll never forget.

Before that trip, I knew from being around June that she had worked a long time for WMU and had a lot of friends. But I'd met her after she retired. As mentor and mentee, I must say the emphasis in our relationship was on me. So until this trip, I really didn't realize some things about June.

For instance, she served as an associate executive director of WMU for many years of her 35-year tenure at WMU. WMU publishes tons of resources for missions organizations of the churches, including groups for the little bitty preschoolers (Mission Friends®), younger girls (Girls in Action®), and teenagers (Acteens®), and so much more.

But that's not all, of course. Through the women's organization, Women on Mission°, literally hundreds of thousands of women are active in missions. WMU relates to missionaries, both here in the United States and those who serve throughout the world. There are two major missions offerings every year, Annie Armstrong Easter Offering® (which provides funds for needs of missionaries in North America), and the Lottie Moon Christmas Offering® (for needs of international missionaries).

People all over the world know and love June Whitlow. And get this: She chose to be my mentor! How cool is that? While we were in St. Louis, I really got a glimpse of what June's life stands for. I knew her to be a kind, loving person and someone who easily gives herself to others. But I had no idea that she was so well known internationally and that she had so many friends.

Really, now, I just felt like I was in the presence of royalty. I know when she reads this, she'll blush and probably chuckle, like she does, and will likely be a little embarrassed, but it's the truth! God blessed me beyond anything I could ever have conceived in my mind when he linked my life to June Whitlow. She deserves so much credit for helping me get from being a struggling woman, a year and a half into recovery with a little baby, to where I am now, a responsible worker and mother.

The most important thing is that in all our time together, she has reflected Jesus Christ. In Galatians 5:22–23, where Paul talks about fruit of the Spirit—that's June Whitlow. And because I see in her what that kind of life looks like, that's how I want to live too. She has shown Christ to me, and He really looks good coming through her!

Being in St. Louis and having the excitement of that meeting gave me a little break from thinking about the failure of the licensure test. I came back determined to study harder and take it again. Life fell back into the usual routine, except that I started getting up at 3:00 A.M. and spending a couple of hours studying before waking Brittany. Sometimes I'd study on my lunch hour and, instead of racing to the day care to pick up Brittany when I got off at 3:00 P.M., I'd go home for an hour and a half or so and study. I was determined to pass.

Next thing I knew, I was getting cards and letters from all over the world. People were writing to encourage me and tell me they were praying for me. June Whitlow again! She had shared with her friends and WMU family that I would be retaking the test and she'd asked them to pray. What an overwhelming outpouring of love I received! People I'd never met or even heard of wrote to say they were praying for me. I got so many letters that I'm sure the mailman must have thought he was delivering mail to somebody really important.

Again, Pathways agreed to pay the $150 test fee, and my mother jumped in to help me have time to study by keeping Brittany on weekends right before the test. I just prayed, *God, help me. You know how I need You now to help me remember all the things I learned in college. Bring it all to the front of my mind, Lord, and help the answers come to me. Help me feel comfortable with all these new procedures I've learned. I'm depending on You, Lord.*

Good news! The second time I passed with a score of 83. I still cry tears of joy right now even thinking about that. Financially, this meant that I immediately became a full-time permanent employee and made significantly more money and had more job security. It also gave me more credibility with my co-workers and patients. But here's the main thing: It gave me an amazing way to testify of God's goodness. I love to tell people about all those things that could have prevented me from ever regaining my license and how, one by one, He took them out of the way or helped me overcome them.

When I talk with women who have lost so much and they think they can't possibly have a rich, full life, or they believe they might never be able to support themselves again, I'm so happy to tell them many things about my life. One of the main things I tell them is how God provided for me to be able to go back to a career I loved but thought I'd lost forever. Praise God for His goodness!

ARRT did make one requirement when issuing my new license. For about a year and a half, I had to have random drug screens. No problem, of course. I did that gladly. At the end of that time, I got a letter notifying me that the drug tests were no longer necessary.

One more blessing came that I never even thought to request. When my license was reinstated, some of my years of previous employment at UAB were also added back. Because of that, I was able to go to an even higher pay grade. I didn't expect this, but what a great way to put icing on the cake, Lord!

So many outstanding things were happening, but there was one more thing I really wanted. I contacted my former DHR worker, Sabrina Bristow, and asked her if we could move toward closing my case with DHR. That would mean I didn't have to be evaluated anymore and there would be no possibility that Brittany could be taken from me. I didn't fear that would ever happen, but I saw ending my contact with DHR as being the next step in being a responsible, independent person.

We had a meeting and I invited all those people who had been working with me through the years. Everyone testified that, indeed, I was able to function as a person and as a mother without supervision from DHR. I was overjoyed when the result of the meeting was announced.

My case was closed.

Chapter 25

OVERWHELMING BLESSINGS

The apartment on Cotton Avenue was transitional housing provided by Pathways. Once I was established in my job and had a steady income, it was time for me to move on and let someone else have that opportunity.

June and I looked at apartments. I wanted to be close to work and church, and we found a beautiful apartment in Homewood, a nice area of Birmingham. The rent was affordable, but there was a big hitch. They required an entire year's rent paid up front because, although I was working on paying bad debts from my past, I hadn't had sufficient time to rebuild my credit.

There was no way I could pay that much money in advance, but June offered—not as a mentor but on her own—to loan me the year's rent. I was extremely grateful. So Brittany and I said good-bye to our little Cotton Avenue apartment, our first home, and settled in our new apartment. I was thrilled to be there. During the next year, I paid my rent to June every month. I was never late and never short on the amount I paid.

About the time we moved, my $500 car wore out and June gave me her Oldsmobile when she bought a new car. Our move meant that we were not convenient to Brittany's day care anymore. June's church, Mountain Brook Baptist, gave us a partial scholarship to their day care. I was so glad for Brittany to be in a Christian environment, but without that scholarship, we certainly wouldn't have been able to afford that. It just made me realize all over again that Brittany is God's child, and He's providing for her all the way. Everything was really looking good for us.

The people of Mountain Brook Baptist have ministered to Brittany and me in many ways through the years, just as Third Presbyterian has. These two churches have taught me how God works through His body, the church, to do His will here on earth. I'll always be grateful for these experiences and for being able to observe and learn what it means to be God's hands and feet on earth.

One huge change that God made in me was the way I managed my money. Of course, on the street the way I managed it was to make a few dollars by whatever means I could — mainly prostitution — and then go to the dope house and spend it.

Managing money had some obstacles even in this new life. UAB wanted to direct deposit my paycheck, so that meant getting a checking account. I didn't think the bank was even going to open an account for me because of my record of bad checks, and going bankrupt years ago. With some research, I found a credit union that would let me open a checking account and arrange for direct deposit of my paycheck.

I also applied for a credit card, thinking I could use it wisely and build my credit rating, but I was turned down. God knew what was best and I trusted in that.

My whole attitude on this was radically different from the old Janet. In times past, I would have screamed and cursed and asked them how dare they deny me anything. Now I was sorry that my past was still keeping me from some things, but I just accepted that God knew when I was ready for all this and He would provide.

I started tithing on my paycheck, giving that portion of earnings back to God's work, and also saving a little bit out of each check. When I left the Cotton Avenue apartment, I received a great surprise. I got a check from Pathways for $1,400! I've already said how Pathways took 30 percent from every paycheck to cover rent and utilities. What I didn't know is that they had also put a small amount in savings from each check. When I became independent of Pathways, they returned that money to me. What a godsend! I used it to make deposits on the utilities at my new apartment, and I bought my first washer and dryer.

While I was still living on Cotton Avenue, I had called Chuck one night and left him a voicemail message. I just wanted to let him know that I was doing well and that I had gone to Olivia's House and finished the Pathways program and was working again. I guess I wanted to let him know, too, how sorry I was for the terrible way I had treated him so many times. He didn't return my call.

The first night I was in the apartment in Homewood, going through boxes and putting things in their place, I was surprised to receive a phone call from Chuck. I told him what had been going on and that I was just getting settled in a new place, one where I was going to be independently responsible. I told him about Brittany and about my job.

He asked if I wanted to take a break and go to a nearby Mexican restaurant for dinner. I agreed to meet him there. I don't know what I expected, and I don't know what Chuck expected. We were both older and wiser. I felt like he might have thought I wanted a second chance with him, but that wasn't my intention. I just wanted a chance to apologize. I had stolen from him and taken advantage of him for years. I wanted him to know that I regretted all those times and that God had become the center of my life. I wanted to ask him for forgiveness.

During dinner, he pulled out a little topaz ring and gave it to me. He had given me that ring years ago and was having it sized when I ran away from him the last time. Now, he still wanted me to have it. "Maybe you won't pawn it," he said. I still have that ring. Chuck had always given me nice things, but I took them for granted. I pawned or sold everything he ever gave me and used the money to buy drugs.

I didn't hear from Chuck again for a long time. We'd connected from time to time over a lot of years, but now there was no lust involved. In years past, it seemed like the only way I could be complete was to sleep with a man or to be a man's property. But knowing that I could relate to Chuck as a friend now was just one of many times the Lord was going to show me about how He had changed my life.

Brittany and I were extremely happy in that Homewood apartment. I took great pride in being able to pay my way with my earnings. I would write out checks for my utilities, insurance, day care, and my tithe. Usually I'd have a little left to contribute to some of the ministries that had sent me their literature when I was in Olivia's House and so hungry to read Christian publications.

Even now, it still is wonderful to be able to get a bill and sit down and write a check to pay it. Or to go for a doctor's appointment and have money for the copay, or to go to the store and buy laundry detergent and toilet paper and all our necessities. To have money for gas in the car and to buy the groceries we need. All of this continues to amaze me. I'm not out there on the street, begging and pleading, desperate and homeless.

Although life was full of joy, there were still some challenges. When Brittany was little and realizing that other children had mamas and daddies in their homes, she'd ask me why she didn't have a daddy. Truth was, I didn't know who her father was. About the time I got pregnant, Tom and I were together a lot but I was with any number of men besides him, so I had no way of knowing. Tom was still getting in touch with me now and then. Several times he went to rehab, but each time he would fall back and use again.

Sometimes Brittany would say to me, "We're not a real family because we don't have a daddy at home." Of course, that broke my heart. I'd try to explain our situation to her and then, when she'd be in bed asleep, I'd cry for her loss and pray for God's guidance.

June, Pat, and I discussed this at length. Both of them thought we should have a paternity test. Tom agreed to do it, so we went together and had the test done. It was quite expensive, about $600 as I remember, but June thought it was important and she paid for it. The test was positive. Tom is Brittany's father.

Tom has been in and out of recovery a few times. Sometimes he stays clean for months at a time and then falls back into using. I know he loves Brittany and wants the best for her and for me. He works part-time and occasionally visits Brittany. I'm always there with them, but I believe she has a right to know he's her father, and he has a right to be with her.

Regardless of what Tom and I had done in our past or what we'd experienced in that sick, sinful relationship, we now have a beautiful little girl. I pray every day that Tom will be successful in recovery and be a daddy that Brittany can admire. In the meantime, God has placed many loving, caring Christian people in our lives, and I know any void will be filled by God Himself and His people.

As each year passes, I tell Brittany more about my past. I don't want to keep secrets from her, and I don't want her to be ashamed of who I am and who she is. I want her to know and fully understand that God has a plan for our lives and that He redeemed us from a horrible situation.

Being a parent is such a serious role. When Brittany was born, I didn't know even the most basic things about taking care of her. The people at Olivia's House helped me greatly. I wanted to learn and wanted to do my best for her. I just didn't have any background to know what to do. I pray to God continually to help me be a godly mother. I tell Him, *God, You know I've never done this before and I don't know how to handle things.*

I ask the Lord to help me every step of the way, to teach me and correct me when I'm wrong, to help me not make mistakes or do permanent damage in what I do as she grows into a teenager and a young woman. The only way I'll know how is to allow Him to lead and guide me through it. I go to Him for everything, and I believe He will never let that change.

Although my new life was full of work and responsibilities, it was also full of lighthearted times too. Growing up, my family had never taken vacations, but during the past few years, June and Pat have taken Brittany and me on several vacations.

Our first trip together was to Florida for four days. We stayed in a beautiful condo and gathered shells on the beach. Brittany was about three by then and she really loved having the waves wash up on her toes. She giggled and giggled. We ate out in wonderful seafood restaurants and rode around looking at the funny houses up on stilts. I'd never seen that part of the country before and I was fascinated.

The next year, June and Pat took us to Disney World in Orlando, Florida. Oh, my! I sat in front of the Cinderella house and watched Mickey Mouse and Snow White and all of the dwarfs singing and dancing around. I was so filled up inside. Can you really picture this? Me, Janet, sitting there with my sweet little girl and seeing her delight in all that was going on. In a way, I think I was going back in time and being a little girl again myself. I'd never been that little girl because I'd wanted to grow up fast and live fast. The trip was just the best time.

Brittany and I would never get to do all these things except for June and Pat. I still feel like I'm living in a dream. When you live in hopelessness, Satan makes you think you will never have any life other than what you're living at the time, but God always has a better plan. For God to pull me out of that and put me in this other world — there are no words to describe what I feel.

In the past few years, I've gotten so many invitations and opportunities to speak and to tell God's story. I've gone with June to speak to WMU groups at national conventions and state conventions. Several magazines have written stories about me, and a Catholic Family Services publication wrote an article about the little boy that I placed for adoption with them.

Pathways and United Way have also given me many opportunities to speak. These are secular organizations, but I always tell the story the same way. I tell about God's redemption and transformation in my life. It's my testimony of how God took a low-down, nasty, filthy, drug-addicted, alcoholic prostitute and gave her a new life with Him.

I've spoken at numerous AA and NA groups and at rehab centers and hospitals. I really love doing that because I like to encourage people who are taking their first steps toward a new life. I always tell them that God didn't intend this new life only for Janet. He wants new life for everyone who will hear His call and respond to Him. He wants to do for everyone exactly what He did for me, and what He keeps doing for me every day of my life now. It's the story of true grace and mercy and love.

For me, it's the highest privilege—indeed, honor—to be asked to speak for Him. Every time I do, right before I begin, I find a quiet place and ask Him once again to use me and to speak through me to tell whatever He wants this particular group to hear. He never disappoints me. I just say, *Lord God, this is Your message. It's got nothing to do with me. It's for Your glory and honor. It's Your time to be exalted and seen and heard. Lord, fill my mouth with Your message. Let them see Your face and hear Your voice, not mine.* That's what I pray, and He always does it.

I still work for UAB, a wonderful employer, and I love my job. My supervisor and co-workers have been so supportive of me. In April 2006, I had the honor of being chosen Employee of the Month. That was a huge moment for me, but at the end of the year, it got even better. I can hardly believe it myself, but out of more than 18,000 employees I was chosen Employee of the Year! All I could think about was how far God had brought me in six short years.

UAB gave a reception in my honor, and Brittany and I rode in the 2006 homecoming parade. I also received a $1,000 cash award and tickets for a concert at the Alys Stephens Center. Now, if nothing else, getting those tickets shows God's sense of humor! The Alys Stephens Center was where I'd hung out and panhandled concertgoers. Now here I was, sitting at the concert among those fine people I would have conned a few short years earlier!

When I gave my acceptance speech at the reception, I told everyone that I was not the one standing there listening to that applause. God was standing there in my body. "You didn't nominate me; you nominated He Who lives in me. God changed me from a dumpster-diving crack addict and prostitute to Employee of the Year!" It was God's honor that day, not mine.

Changes are taking place all the time. Brittany is growing and thriving. She is a sweet girl and a good student. I'm proud of her, and I'm still asking the Lord to guide me as I try to raise His girl for Him.

In 2008, I bought a townhouse near June and Pat. The woman who used to sleep in deserted basements or beg her druggie friends to let her spend the night now has a townhouse of her own!

We still go on vacations with June and Pat, and we go to church together. They are Brittany's Grandma June and Aunt Pat. I can't imagine what my life would be without them. When I think about how God brought June and me together from such radically different backgrounds, I'm astounded to think what a magnificent plan He had in place. Coincidence? No way!

I try to volunteer and help people who are struggling with the same problems I battled. Being their judge isn't my responsibility because I realize how many times I could have changed and didn't. I certainly don't ever want them to think that I have any pride in myself because of the changes in my life. All the glory for that goes to God alone.

It's been my great pleasure to be able to teach some classes at Olivia's House, the treatment center where I was a client, and to spend time with the women there. I gather donations for clothes, toys, and household items to give to them. I don't think there's anyone in Birmingham, Alabama, who doesn't know that Janet will come and get their donations and take them to Olivia's House or Pathways.

Sometimes I'm asked what I want for Brittany's future. My prayers for her can be summed up very simply. I want her to be pure and holy and completely dedicated to God. I pray that she won't make the same mistakes I've made. I talk often with her about what it means to put God first in her life, because I failed to do that until the day she was born—and I was born again.

There are simply no words to describe how much Brittany means to me and how proud I am of her. I think back now to the hours of her birth and how God knew He was giving me such a precious gift, even when my heart was rebelling there in the delivery room. In an instant, when God gave me His love, He also gave me an extraordinary love for my baby girl.

Brittany has filled my life with so much joy. She makes splendid grades and loves drama and music. She truly blesses me every day just by being herself. I also see her growing in her faith. I am trusting that God will grow her into a young woman who loves Him and lives for Him.

In the months when we were finishing the writing of this book, my mother became ill. I began to notice that she was so easily fatigued, and I urged her to see a doctor. On July 13, 2011, she was diagnosed with lung cancer and on August 28, she went to be with the Lord.

Those weeks with her in the hospital were precious and painful at the same time. I didn't want to see her suffer, but I didn't want to let her go, either. I knew my mother had given her heart to the Lord several years ago, so I knew where she would go, but after all the years of our broken relationship, I wanted more years to enjoy being together.

I'll forever be grateful that we had 11½ good years together. I have so many wonderful memories of those years. Staying with her on weekend passes and enjoying drinking coffee and eating those big breakfasts she loved to make for me. Seeing Mom and Brittany together, playing and just loving each other. Laughing, praying, talking, sharing. My heart is heavy that she is not here with us, but my heart sings with the thought of spending eternity in heaven with her.

Brittany and I will continue to miss her. I wish she could know that this book will bring comfort to many mothers just like her who love their wayward children. I know she would encourage other mothers and fathers to stay strong and keep the faith that the Lord will bring healing to their families just as He did to ours.

My brother, Stan, and I have a good brother and sister relationship.

My first son, David, is married and has three beautiful children. I'm proud of how he's trying to live his life for God. I enjoy being with him and his family as much as possible.

Every year, I get a picture and some news about the little boy I placed through Catholic Family Services. He is 19 now. He loves to play the piano but struggles with geometry. How I would love to hear him play his piano. Who knows what will happen in the future? Maybe I'll have the chance to meet this son some day.

I have no idea where Brandon is, the son that was taken from me by DHR. I pray every day for him and for my other children, that God will protect them and keep them in safe, loving homes. I also pray that none of my children travel the low road that I did.

It's my heart's desire that one day my children, grandchildren, and I could all sit around a big old table and have Christmas dinner together. I'll tell them God's story of how He rescued me and gave me new life. I'll ask their forgiveness for not being the mother I should have been. I'll tell them how much I've prayed for them through the years.

Maybe this dream will come true here on earth, but, if not, I'll continue to pray for God to protect them all and bring us together in heaven. To God be the glory!

EPILOGUE

So that's my story—God's story, that is. Although I can't know each reader personally, I have been praying for you as you read about the amazing way God rescued me from a desperate life of sin and changed me completely. Please don't think I'm bragging. No way! I know I'm nothing without God and I don't ever forget that.

I don't know why you chose to read this book, but I pray that it's touched your heart. I hope you've never lived the way I have, and I hope no one in your family is involved in such a troubled lifestyle. Whether or not you or anyone in your family has been involved in the things I've described, please pray for the literally thousands of people who live on the streets and hustle for food and shelter. Truth is, of course, many of them are hustling for the pills and drinks and drugs that mean much more to them than a good meal or a soft bed.

Your prayers are important. We may not see results, but be faithful. You don't need to know names. Just pray. God knows the names.

❀ ❀ ❀

A note to loved ones

Perhaps you're a parent, grandparent, brother, sister, uncle, or aunt of someone who's lost in sin and living on the street, as I did. Maybe your loved one is in bondage and addiction to alcohol or drugs and you don't know how to help.

Don't give up! I hope you read this book and say, "If God can do that in Janet's life, surely He can do it for . . ." Yes, He can!

If you're watching a loved one self-destruct, I know you're tired, physically and emotionally. You may also be financially devastated. My mother wore out with me too. She took me in time after time only to see me fall back to the old ways again. I'm thankful she lived to see God change me and to become my friend as well as my mother. I'm grateful that Brittany knew the love of a grandmother.

I wish I had the magic answer for you, a sure-fire formula for bringing your loved one out of the pit of hell, but I don't. There are a few things I can tell you, so here goes:

The choices your child has made are not your fault. Most parents of a wayward child blame themselves. If I'd been a better parent, if I hadn't gotten a divorce, if I had been more supportive. The "ifs" can go on forever. Yes, you probably made some mistakes in parenting, but Satan loves nothing more than seeing you drowning in guilt. The truth is, we all make our own choices, and your child is responsible for his or her own decisions.

Parents want to believe that if they give a child just one more chance, they'll straighten up. So you bail them out, give them money, let them come home, and hope for the best. If you've done that one time or two times, good for you! We all need someone who will give us a break and a second chance.

But if you've done that until you can't count the times, it's time to quit. They may have to spend some time in jail or go without a good meal or struggle for a place to sleep. I know that breaks your heart, but sometimes parents have to step out of the picture and let God work.

I've heard people say that addicts must hit rock bottom before they look up. Well, what's rock bottom? I don't know, and I think it's different for every person. If your child is addicted to drugs or alcohol, that craving is more important than anything else in the world. I'm sorry to say it, but to them it's more important than you are.

If they need a good meal or a shower and a change of clothes, by all means, give that to them. But if they've used you again and again, it's probably time for tough love.

And, yes, I know that the one you love may come to a tragic end. I've seen it happen many times. I could have died of an overdose or an injury. I could have been murdered. Why I didn't die of AIDS or any number of diseases, I don't know, except that

I know God protected me. Pray for protection for your child, but if the worst happens, know that you did your best and that we can't judge the heart and soul of another person.

Express your love to them and let them know you're praying for them. And then pray. I truly believe in the power of prayer. Many people prayed for me through the years. I can't explain how God got through to me in that delivery room when I was screaming and using His name in vain, but He did. Pray for God to intervene in your child's life, and pray for that child to be ready to receive Him.

I don't know your name, but I'm praying for you to be able to trust in God and continue to be strong. I know that God blesses those who honor Him.

A message for those who want forgiveness
If you're reading this book and you're living the life of addiction and sin that I did, or if—Praise God!—you're in a treatment center, there are so many things I want to say to you. I wish I could reach out from these pages and gather you in my arms. I want you to know that God can change your life just as He changed mine. You may not be able to believe that right now, but it's true.

Maybe someone gave you this book as a warning about what could happen in your life if you keep on the road you're on right now. If you're living in bondage, I beg you to realize what God can do with your life if you're willing to let Him change you. The truth is that sin feels pretty good when we're in the middle of it. If it didn't, we wouldn't do it. When you're doped out on crack, you're feeling good. When you're drunk as a skunk and having a high old time with your drinking friends, yeah, that's fun for the moment. And when you fall in bed with a complete stranger who's telling you how beautiful you are and saying and doing all the right things to give you a night's pleasure, that feels really good too.

But what about when it's over? What about when you wake up and don't even know the name of the person in bed with you? Or when your cravings are so powerful that they take over your life and the only important thing is the next drink or the next hit? Then it's not so much fun. Maybe you have a few moments when you're not drunk or high and you realize just how dirty and evil your life has become.

The hardest thing in the world is to believe that God forgives. At different times in my life, people tried to tell me about God's forgiveness, but I just couldn't believe it. I had done so many, many horrible things, and Satan had me believing that even if I wanted to know God and ask for His forgiveness, it wasn't possible.

After all, how could He forgive me for abortion, adultery, lying, cheating, stealing, drunkenness, cursing, ranting, panhandling, mistreating people, pimping other girls, using people, multiple sex partners, selling my body for such little bits of money to buy my drugs, even stealing from the church and God's people? How could He ever forgive all that?

Satan would whisper in my ear: *You've done too much. Nobody wants you. Nobody will love you. Do what you want to do, what feels good, because that's as good as it's ever going to get for you, Janet.* And I believed all that.

I believed it until November 11, 2000, when God Himself whispered a different message into my heart, when He touched me in a way that I couldn't fail to know it was Him. That's when His forgiveness washed over me and made me new.

As I write this part, I'm completely overwhelmed by His goodness and mercy to me, and I thank Him for His total forgiveness. I thank Him for loving me all those years when I cursed Him and spit in His face. I threw the stones. I shoved the crown of thorns on His head. And I was among those who yelled out, "Crucify Him! Crucify Him!"

But do you know what Jesus said? "Father, please forgive Janet. She doesn't know what she's doing. I'm not going to let her go, so please forgive her, Father." And praise His holy name, He spared me until I did turn to Him. I keep saying the same thing, but I mean it. I'm so thankful. I'm just so thankful.

The depths of His forgiveness are unimaginable. I know with everything that is within me that He forgave me. When I let Him into my heart, He covered me with His righteousness and He blotted out all my sin. His Word says that He put my sin as far from Him as the East is from the West. That's pretty amazing, isn't it?

Today I can walk with my head up, unashamed, without regret, not taking revenge, or holding resentments. I'm moving forward in the newness He gave me. You see, God sent His Son to die a wretched death on a cross to pay for my sins. In that moment, my sins were draped on Jesus and His death paid the penalty for all of them.

But here's the good news for you: In that instant, He paid for your sins too. All you have to do is receive forgiveness and believe. You may not have a dramatic Jesus moment like I did, but when you release your heart to Him, your salvation and freedom from sin will be every bit as real as mine.

I pray that reading this book and thinking on what I'm telling you will be that decision time for you. Don't think for a second that you've done too much for Him to forgive. The truth is that we are all sinners when we come into this world. The Bible tells us that "all have sinned, and come short of the glory of God" (Romans 3:23 KJV). None of us can ever be so good that we don't need God's forgiveness.

Sometimes I look at my Christian friends, those who have been Christians most of their lives and who live for Jesus so completely. When I first began to meet people like them, I wondered if they needed God's forgiveness. Of course, they did! I think about June Whitlow, who is the most perfect woman I've ever met. I also think about Ted Pearson, who gives himself totally to serving God through helping people who use and abuse him again and again. I can name many others. But the Bible says we all are sinners and need God's forgiveness.

The other thing that people like me find difficult to believe is that God really loves us. *He loves me?* Yes, He does. "But God shows his love for us in that while we were yet sinners Christ died for us" (Romans 5:8 KJV). We didn't have to "get good" first for Him to love us. He already loved us. In the deepest pit of the most despicable sin, He loved us. Incredible!

Our sin would condemn us to eternal hell, but because of God's love, He provided salvation for us by sending His Son, Jesus, to die on the Cross. Even if they've never been in church, most people know a few Bible verses, and this one may be familiar to you: "For God so loved the world that he gave his only Son, that whoever believes in him should not perish but have eternal life" (John 3:16 RSV). We don't have to die in our sin! We don't have to spend eternity in hell! Because of His love for us, we have a choice.

We can choose to love God and believe in Him. That's all it takes! It sounds too easy and simple, doesn't it? The Bible says, "If you confess with your mouth that Jesus is Lord and believe in your heart that God raised him from the dead, you will be saved" (Romans 10:9). You must believe in your heart and then you must tell God that you're trusting Him with your life, and you will be saved from the wrath of hell.

"Therefore, if anyone is in Christ, he is a new creation. The old has passed away; behold, the new has come" (2 Corinthians 5:17 ESV). That means that when I accepted Christ as my Savior, I became a different person. I still looked like the same old Janet, but my heart was completely different. I didn't want to do all those things I did before.

Does being saved mean we'll never sin again? Oh, heavens, no. But it means I've already been forgiven for those sins, and it also means I don't want to sin any more. And when I do mess up, the Holy Spirit, Who now lives in my heart, convicts me of sin and it grieves me to know that I've sinned.

My sins now are not the sins of my past. I don't get drunk or high, and I don't sleep around anymore. My sins now are more about thoughts that are not pure, resenting, or coveting, perhaps gossiping or being unkind. You may think, *well, those are not bad sins, nothing like abortion or adultery,* for instance. To God, sin is sin. My greatest desire every day is to grow more and more like Jesus, who was perfect. I'll never be perfect. There's no danger of that! But in every way possible, I want to let the light of Jesus' love flow through me.

So if you've read this book and you want a change in your life, God can change you! He's just waiting for you to come to Him. He's calling you. It's not only your actions that will change. No, you won't want to do all those dirty sins anymore, but living for Jesus means more than just not doing wrong things. It means knowing that God's Holy Spirit lives in your heart. He will comfort you when you need it, He'll guide you in making decisions and resisting temptations, and He'll give you the reassurance that when you die on this earth, you'll live with Him in heaven forever.

If you want that to happen in your life, simply pray to God. Admit your sins—He wants to hear you confess!—and ask His forgiveness. Tell Him you are committing your life to Him and want to live for Him every moment. Ask Him to guide you and help you as you begin your new life.

If you don't have a church you regularly attend, visit some churches and see where God would have you serve. Yes, serve. Once you've known the forgiveness of God and received a new life, you'll want to help others know that. You'll want to give to others. Make an appointment with a pastor and express what God has done for you. Go to church and make some friends, ones who share your new faith and will help you grow stronger.

For Brittany Anne

As I write these words, Brittany's 12th birthday is only a few days away. It's my birthday, too, the day I was born again. On that day, November 11, 2000, Brittany and I were both delivered. She was delivered into my arms and we began a journey together. I was delivered—praise His name!—from the existence I called living for so many years and into the arms of my Savior, Jesus Christ.

Much has happened in these 12 years. Brittany and I have a wonderful life. We laugh a lot and have great times together. We have our crying times, too, but we work it all out.

Recently, I had the great joy of seeing Brittany make a profession of faith in Jesus. Saying that I am thankful doesn't even touch what I feel about that. I pray every day that God will protect her and teach her and lead her to follow Him as she grows into young womanhood, and I pray she never will experience the kind of life I had before I came to love the Lord.

I came to believe in God as I traveled a difficult road. As I've told this story of His grace, I have thought about what others may think or say. Mostly, however, I am thanking God for allowing me to come to Him, and for His gracious gifts. And I am hoping that others reading this will allow God to change their life. After all, He made all things and everything belongs to Him! I pray also for my daughter — who is first God's girl — that others will see how the old is gone and all things have been made new; there is nothing to fear or to be ashamed of for me, or for Brittany. I have been made new and I and Brittany are blessed indeed. I have new life and such a precious daughter, whom I love entirely. I love you, Brit!

What's your story?

I would love to meet you and hear your story. I'd love to put my arms around you and tell you how I've prayed for you. The truth is, we may never meet on earth, but if you have Jesus as your Savior, then you're my sister or brother. And the best part is that someday we will meet in heaven.

Dear friend, believe it. When all the saints go marching in, we'll be there! Hallelujah and praise God!

Experience the free online Book Club Discussion Guide for **Delivered**.

Get more out of your reading experience with the free online Book Discussion Guide for *Delivered* at NewHopeDigital.com.

Resources to Help
Awaken the Calling
to Love God and Love Others!

Compelled
Living the Mission of God
ISBN-13: 978-1-59669-351-7
N124104 · $14.99

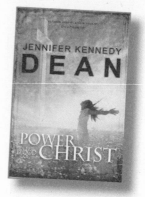

Power in the Blood of Christ
ISBN-13: 978-1-59669-363-0
N134106 · $14.99

Thirst No More
A One-Year Devotional Journey
ISBN-13: 978-1-59669-312-8
N114146 · $12.99

Hunger No More
A One-Year Devotional Journey
Through the Psalms
ISBN-13: 978-1-59669-355-5
N124108 · $12.99